From Reflection to Action:
A Choosing to Participate Toolkit

FACING
HISTORY
AND
OURSELVES

Facing History and Ourselves
16 Hurd Road
Brookline, MA 02445
www.facinghistory.org

1 2 3 4 5 6 7 8 9 10

ISBN 978-1-940457-45-1

Contents

How to Use This Guide

From Reflection to Action: A Choosing to Participate Toolkit is designed to support Facing History educators who are implementing Facing History content and pedagogy in the classroom. While many Facing History units and case studies include a Choosing to Participate (CTP) chapter, the resources included here provide a flexible collection of activities, readings, lessons, and strategies that can be used alone or in combination to develop a civic action experience that meets the specific curriculum objectives and time available in your classroom.

Students develop and strengthen their "participation muscles"—a combination of civic skills, knowledge, and dispositions—throughout the course of their time in school. This guide provides a range of ways to do this that can build on each other over time, which is particularly valuable when Facing History units are implemented in different courses and grades within a school or district. In addition, the sample projects and assignments illustrate how teachers can structure their Facing History unit to meet the growing requirement to complete student civic action projects, grounded in the historical context and reflection practice that Facing History has found leads to the most meaningful and long-lasting experience for students.

Developing Civic Agency through History and Literature

Facing History and Ourselves believes the paramount purpose of education is to prepare students to be active and thoughtful participants in democracy. Through Facing History's units and case studies, students learn that history is the product of the choices made by people in the past—and they learn the power of their own choice to participate today. Every Facing History unit is built around a common structure—what we call our journey—which organizes the inquiry and shapes the journey that students and teachers will take together.

The scope and sequence begins with what students know and care most about: themselves and the social world they inhabit. Students probe themes of identity, individuality, conformity, stereotyping, group loyalty, and responsibilities to those beyond their immediate circle. They then expand their thinking about these topics as they investigate a deep case study in history or literature. Through a wide range of individual and group activities designed to promote students' historical understanding, critical thinking, and civic agency and engagement—as well as an ongoing practice of self-reflection—they explore how society influences individuals and, ultimately, how individuals can influence and impact their society.

Facing History's approach helps students understand that progress toward a more just, equitable, and inclusive society has never been inevitable; rather, it is the result of the choices of individuals and groups. Students learn that participating in a democracy involves many small choices and decisions as much as it does ambitious acts and social movements. Facing History student Parima K. from Watchung Hills Regional High School in New Jersey summed up the approach and its impact on her:

> When you *study* history, you might be learning the facts, learning dates, but when you *face* history, you're absorbing what it meant for the people who experienced them and applying it to your own life when you go forward and have to make choices and make decisions.

The Facing History Journey

Choosing to Participate

Connecting the complexities of the past with the issues of today to help students understand that they have the power to impact society and the future through individual and group actions.

Individual & Society

How individual and group identities are formed, and how these identities influence behavior and decision-making.

We & They

The processes that help people connect but also contribute to misunderstanding, stereotyping, and conflict. The ways in which membership can be a tool for constructive *and* destructive purposes.

Judgment, Memory & Legacy

How communities and nations respond to mass violence and injustice. Reflections on questions of guilt and accountability, reparations for those who were victimized, and how a community or nation can move forward.

Case Study

A case study that includes an exploration of the small steps, individual choices, and range of human behavior that led to times of discrimination, segregation, or mass violence in history or literature.

Building the Foundation for Civic Action

Increasingly, the world of civic education is oriented around action, an approach of learning-by-doing that leads students to develop civic knowledge and skills through projects and experiences in their own communities in order to become active and thoughtful civic participants. At Facing History, we understand that effective "action civics" depends not only on providing civic education—grounded in the study of history and literature—that nurtures students' capacity for *both* reflection and action but also on supporting four other essential practices of civic education, which Facing History infuses throughout our resources and pedagogical approach.

- **Civic education begins in learner-centered classrooms that value students' identities.**

  Our thematic focus on individual and group identity centers and validates students' multiple identities and personal experiences, a practice that promotes both academic and civic learning.

- **Civic education must confront bias and develop a sense of the common good.**

  It's essential for students to understand the systems and institutions that structure how citizens engage with government. But a healthy civic life also depends on how citizens relate to *each other*. Empathy, respect, and perspective-taking are not only social-emotional skills but also key qualities of good citizenship, because they support students' ability to imagine and act on a notion of the common good.

- **Civic education must engage with the complexities of history.**

  History is essential to civic education because it illuminates key aspects of democracy that are missing when the functions of government are taught in the abstract. Our case studies demonstrate, first and foremost, the fragility of democracy itself. They invite students to probe the gaps between the ideals in America's founding documents and the history and lived realities of injustice and systemic bias—an approach that has been shown to stimulate young people's civic engagement.

- **Civic education must introduce current events and controversial issues.**

  Current events introduce the issues, dilemmas, and controversies that shape civic life today and empower students to make informed and meaningful choices as citizens. Just as important as helping students understand the issues in the headlines is supporting them and encouraging practice in democratic deliberation over topics that divide society. Without opportunities to engage in difficult conversations across differences at school, students may never learn this essential civic skill—or they will take their cues from cable news and social media.

These practices stimulate the authentic motivation that is essential to a meaningful civic action project. They also support equity, encouraging self-reflection on how students' own identities, experiences, and assumptions shape their civic efforts—as well as building awareness of how equitably opportunities and resources are distributed and which voices are centered in civic actions. Finally, these practices help students develop the knowledge, agency, and capacity for ethical reflection that make any civic action project successful.

From Reflection to Action

"Choosing to Participate" is the final step in Facing History's scope and sequence, as described on the previous pages. It is the section of a Facing History unit or course where students **reflect**—and **act**—on their growing sense of voice and agency, which they have been developing, practicing, and applying throughout the journey. By reflecting on the connections between past and present, students consider how they can apply the lessons of upstanders in history in order to bring about a more just, equitable, and inclusive society today. And they examine and implement decisions—from small everyday actions to independent civic action projects, long-term commitments, and everything in between—that allow them to begin that work.

Scholar George Lipsitz explains what he hopes students, informed by a rigorous study of history, will think when confronted with present-day injustice:

> We know this place; we've been here before. We come from a tradition. People of all colors and all races come from a tradition of social justice in which ordinary men and women thought it was worth risking everything to create a fair and democratic society.

Ultimately, Facing History and Ourselves hopes to create a society of thoughtful citizens who think deeply about the way they live—when they are riding the subway to work as much as when they hear about incidents of mass violence that demand a global response. Indeed, at the conclusion of the Facing History journey, we hope that students will believe that their choices *do* matter and will feel compelled to think carefully about the decisions they make, realizing that their choices will ultimately shape the world.

Moving from Bystander to Upstander

"I grew up believing that because I was female, because I was Latina, my voice was never meant to be heard. The courage of these survivors made me realize that not using your voice is a choice, no matter what you've been through. . . . Standing by is a choice. I know that now. If we could teach that to every student, the younger the better . . . just imagine how quickly the world might change."

—Emily C., recipient of the 2018 New York Student Upstander Award, recalling the impact of three Holocaust survivors who visited her Facing History class

---

The Role of Reflection

One thing that all Choosing to Participate units and activities (as well as Facing History resources) have in common is an emphasis on ongoing self-reflection. Reflection provides the opportunity for students to draw upon their identities and lived experiences, make connections to the content they are learning, document the evolution of their projects and thinking, and apply what they've learned to issues that are meaningful to their lives.

In order for a civic participation project or activity to feel personally relevant and be successful, it is important to build in multiple opportunities to reflect (both silently and in conversation with peers)—not just at the beginning and end of a project but throughout the process. This allows students to revisit on their thinking and better understand how it is evolving and will continue to evolve. In this way, they develop the practice of self-reflection and questioning, key skills in understanding and taking responsibility for their learning throughout their education. For this reason, many educators build in a regular journaling practice at the beginning of the school year. (For more information on journaling, see the Journals in a Facing History Classroom teaching strategy at facinghistory.org/ctp-links.)

The Impact of Reflection

Deztinee G., a junior at Whitney M. Young Magnet High School in Chicago and a member of the Facing History Student Leadership Team (at the time of this speech), addressed the impact of questioning and self-reflection during her Ethnic Studies class:

"Aside from learning about the world, [this class] gave me the opportunity to learn more about myself. . . . As I asked more questions and reflected upon myself . . . , my perspective changed. What matters is not just the resources I have, but what I choose to do with them.

"I created a social justice group called Radical Goons. There are about 15 of us involved. We started with an idea to provide 'Know Your Rights' workshops for middle schoolers. But as we dug into the issues around immigration, we realized there are so many other issues that need to be addressed. We're just getting started, but we hope to give workshops to middle and high school students that touch on self-care, racism, and mental health."

Taking Action

Students do not become effective civic actors with the flip of a switch or through one civic action project. Students' civic engagement and sense of civic agency is developed and practiced over time, both in and out of the classroom. We often think about civic participation as a matter of politics, activism, and voting, and all of these activities are essential to supporting a strong democracy. But these are not the only ways of choosing to participate.

The news from around the world can be overwhelming, and young people often wonder how they can possibly bring about the change they seek. The goal of implementing a Choosing to Participate (CTP) lesson or unit is not to force students to take action. Instead, its aim is to open their eyes to the many different ways of participating, past and present; to the civic and political knowledge they have gained or observed through their lived experience; and to the tools that others have used—or that they have access to—to make positive changes in their communities, country, and the world overall.

Scholar Ethan Zuckerman, who studies civic engagement around the world, has noticed a trend toward types of civic action that do not rely on the power of government and other institutions to make change, including creative uses of art and technology, the formation of small businesses, and attempts to influence the norms and traditions of communities and cultures. Zuckerman concludes:

> If you feel like you can change the world through elections, through our political system, through the institutions we have—that's fantastic, so long as you're engaged in making change. If you mistrust those institutions and feel disempowered by them, . . . I challenge you to find ways you can make change through code [technology], through markets, through norms [unspoken rules], through becoming a fierce and engaged monitor of the institutions we have and that we'll build. The one stance that's not acceptable, as far as I'm concerned[,] is that of disengagement, of deciding that you're powerless and remaining that way.[1]

A Flexible Model to Support Students' Civic Participation

Depending on your grade, unit, curriculum objectives, and time available, Choosing to Participate provides a flexible model of reflection and action that can range from one class period at the end of a Facing History unit to a semester-long elective or independent civic action project.

On the pages that follow, you will find a range of resources, teaching strategies, activities, and lessons that you can use to develop your CTP experience.

The following table provides a brief summary of these resources, along with how or when you may want to use them.

Then, beginning on page 86, we have included some specific project examples from a range of Facing History schools, including independent senior civic action projects and actual assignments materials.

---

1   Ethan Zuckerman, "Insurrectionist Civics in the Age of Mistrust," . . . *My heart's in Accra* (blog), entry posted October 19, 2015, accessed October 29, 2015.

Resources at a Glance

Reflection

These resources include reflection activities that can be used to launch or complete Choosing to Participate (CTP) activities and civic action projects; stimuli that can be used for journaling or with the Big Paper: Building a Silent Conversation or Learn to Listen, Listen to Learn teaching strategies (see facinghistory.org/ctp-links); and readings and videos that provide examples of upstanders, both historic and current.

Civic Self-Portrait *Duration: 1–2 class periods*	Students reflect on and apply what they have learned through their study of social change movements and upstanders to define the kind of civic actor they want to be in the world. This activity helps students think about and visualize the different elements of being a civic participant. It can be used in conjunction with journaling to provide a visual representation of their civic skills, values, and identity as they begin a civic action project.	Page 16
Walking with the Wind: The Power of Persistence *Duration: 1 class period*	This lesson, which can be used to kick off or complete a CTP activity or unit, encourages students to reflect on our responsibilities to participate and persist together in the process of creating a more just and equitable society.	Page 19
Sample Reflection Questions	These reflection questions can be used or adapted for journaling prompts or small-group and class discussion.	Page 23
Suggested Quotations for Reflection	These quotations can be used for journaling to help students reflect on the content you have been studying; students can choose from a curated set of options for written or oral reflections; or you can use several of the quotations as stimuli for Big Paper silent conversations.	Page 25
Choosing to Participate Readings	These readings provide examples of individuals or groups who have chosen to speak out or take action. Assign individual readings or use as part of the Jigsaw: Developing Community and Disseminating Knowledge strategy to help students explore what it means to participate (if you have limited time, this can be a culminating CTP activity for your unit, paired with the Civic Self-Portrait activity or a cCulminating Reflection Routine). You can also use these readings for levers of power analyses, or you can curate other readings and ask students to bring in articles about individuals who they consider to be upstanders today.	Page 28
Brainstorming Strategies	These strategies can be used to brainstorm small-group and class projects and expand student self-reflection by engaging in dialogue with a community of learners.	Page 40
Culminating Reflection Routines	These reflection routines underscore the idea that civic participation is an ongoing process and help students consider how they will apply what they have learned as they move forward. The reflections can be used to lock in the learning upon completion of a CTP experience or civic action project.	Page 41

Action

These resources include lessons and activities that provide a structured process for implementing a CTP project, which can be useful if you have limited time. Leveraging Civic Power and 10 Questions for Young Changemakers can be used either as standalone experiences or as part of a larger civic action project.

Public Memory and the Role of Memorials *Duration: 2–4 class periods*	Students consider the impact of history and memory on the present by reflecting on the purposes of memorials and creating one.	Page 44
Building a Toolbox *Duration: 1–2 class periods*	Students consider the "tools" that individuals, groups, and institutions use to create change and then apply the lessons of the past to their own lives by building a "toolbox" that includes the skills, attitudes, and actions necessary to be an upstander.	Page 56
Leveraging Civic Power *Duration: 1–2 class periods*	Students explore civic power and apply the "levers of power" framework to analyze the accessibility and effectiveness of different strategies for participation.	Page 60
10 Questions for Young Changemakers *Duration: 2+ class periods*	Students learn about and apply the 10 Questions Framework to consider how to develop effective and inclusive participation strategies.	Page 67

Sample CTP Projects and Assignments

While there is no single way to implement Choosing to Participate in the classroom, these examples from Facing History schools can provide inspiration and guidance.

CTP Project Spotlights	These stories provide concrete examples of how CTP has come to life in the classroom and in the lives of students.	Page 80
Sample Assignments from Partner Schools	The following examples come from members of Facing History's Partner Schools Network, made up of over 140 schools that embrace Facing History's core themes as foundational to their mission and weave Facing History content and teaching strategies throughout the entire school: in classes, advisory groups, faculty meetings, and school community activities.	
Final Exhibition Project, 8th-Grade Humanities *Duration: One month*	This final project is the culminating activity of a year-long humanities course focused on the questions: *What does it mean to belong? Who decides if you belong? How do people gain belonging?* It consists of a written element and a presentation (poster and toolbox), as well as research on history and current events. Students present their posters and research at an exhibition night for friends, family, community members, and staff. From Gateway Middle School, San Francisco, CA	Page 87
Independent Social Justice-Themed Art Project, Senior Year *Duration: One semester*	Second-semester seniors complete an independent art project that focuses on a social justice topic of personal interest that they have written a paper about during their first semester. The project is self-directed, self-motivated, and explores how to best communicate their message through an interactive art form. Showcased in an annual Choosing to Participate Final Exhibition for the community. From The Facing History School, New York, NY	Page 96

Group Social Action Project, Senior Year *Duration: Two months*	Students taking the Urban Studies/Ethnic Studies elective course complete an independent social action project and presentation in teams of two to four students, culminating in a presentation to peers, teachers, parents, and community members. From Ánimo Jackie Robinson Charter High School, Los Angeles, CA	Page 98
Independent Social Action Project, Senior Year *Duration: One year*	Seniors take a Civics/Choosing to Participate course and complete independent social action projects (SAP) in their community, culminating in a public presentation at the Senior Exhibition. The goal of these projects is for seniors to learn and practice the skills of active citizenship. From New Haven Academy, New Haven, CT	Page 99

Reflection

Civic Self-Portrait

Materials

 **HANDOUT**
Civic Self-Portrait

Overview

Students reflect on and apply what they have learned through their study of social change movements and upstanders in history and current events. The Civic Self-Portrait helps students think about and visualize the different elements of being a civic participant. You can complete this activity in one class period, or you may want to assign the Civic Self-Portrait as homework so students have more time to reflect and create their visuals.

Procedure

1. Reflect on What Civic Participation Means

Ask students to reflect in their journals:

- What are the most important lessons that you have learned from the choices of upstanders and civic actors? What makes these lessons important to you?

- How can you apply these lessons to your own choices?

Invite some students to share their ideas with the class, listing the important lessons on the board. Then, in a Think, Pair, Share activity, ask students to consider the following questions:

- How do you want to participate in your community and beyond?

- What strengths, talents, and passions do you have that help you think about how you might engage with the world?

2. Students Create Civic Self-Portraits

Distribute copies of the Civic Self-Portrait handout and review the directions. In order to help students begin the project and to build class community around the idea of embracing our roles as civic participants, you might consider modeling the activity by beginning your own Civic Self-Portrait on the board or flip chart. Students can record their ideas directly on the handout, or, to help them think more deeply, first have them reflect in their journals to answer the questions on the handout. Then instruct them to create their Civic Self-Portraits, using ideas from their journal response, symbols and images, and color to envision their civic selves.

3. Debrief

Depending on the amount of time you have available, particularly if students will be completing their handouts as homework, students could share their Civic Self-Portraits in pairs or small groups or in a Gallery Walk. If you are completing this activity at the beginning of a CTP activity or civic action project, you may want to have students revisit their self-portraits at the end of the project or activity to see if they want to change anything as a result of their experiences.

Civic Self-Portrait

Who am I? How do I want to participate?

Directions: Draw a "civic self-portrait" below or on a separate piece of paper. The picture can be as simple as a stick figure or something more complex.

Head
What have I read, heard, or studied this year/unit/week that has made me ask questions about myself or my community?

Eyes
What have I seen that is influencing how I act? What am I looking for?

Ears
What voices, sources, or ideas do I listen to in order to understand what needs to be done?

Mouth
How do I want to use my voice?

Heart
What do I care about? What is my passion?

Stomach
What is my first thought or gut instinct about how to act? What do I worry about?

Hands
How do I want to act with people in my community? Whom do I want to connect with?

Feet
What are my hopes for the future? What are the first steps I can take to get there?

Walking with the Wind: The Power of Persistence

Essential Questions

- What is the importance of persistence when we exercise our civic power?

- What does it take for individuals to strengthen their communities and make a positive difference in the world?

Materials

 **READING**
Walking with the Wind

Overview

You may want to begin or end your unit or CTP activity with a broader reflection on our responsibilities to participate and persist together to create a more just and inclusive society. While that participation may take many forms, one thing is constant: In an imperfect world marked by suffering and injustice, there will always be occasions to act. In our world of soundbites, social media, and multitasking, the need for persistence—and solidarity in the face of fear, uncertainty, and even the feeling of being unequal to the task—cannot be overestimated.

In this lesson, students will explore this idea through an excerpt from Congressman John Lewis's memoir. Congressman Lewis has modeled persistence, engagement, and civic power in his work for a more just world. Born in 1940 to Alabama sharecroppers, Lewis became a civil rights leader in the 1960s and was elected to the US Congress in 1986. In 2013, reflecting on the 50th anniversary of the March on Washington, during the second term of the first African American president, Lewis made it clear that the fight for voting rights continues: "If you ask me whether the election . . . is the fulfillment of Dr. King's dream, I say, 'No, it's just a down payment.' There's still too many people 50 years later . . . that are being left out and left behind."

Procedure

1. **Read and Discuss "Walking with the Wind"**

   Distribute copies of the "Walking with the Wind" reading to students and briefly discuss the life of Congressman John Lewis. Read aloud John Lewis's story and then discuss its meaning with the class. You might also consider using the Text-to-Text, Text-to-Self, Text-to-World teaching strategy.

   - How does John Lewis use the metaphor of "walking with the wind" to talk about the role of a citizen in society? What does his metaphor suggest about what it takes to strengthen communities and make a positive difference in the world?

- Why was it important that "the people of conscience never left the house"?
- What do you think about Lewis's conviction that "another storm would come, and we would have to do it all over again"? What other examples of this sort of persistence have you encountered in your own experience or in the world around you? How do we sustain our commitment to issues we care about?

2. Reflect in Student Journals

Ask students to write a reflection in their journals in response to the class discussion and the following question: What does choosing to participate mean to you? In what ways might you participate in the communities around you?

Walking with the Wind

As a young student, John Lewis worked with Dr. Martin Luther King Jr. and became a key leader of the civil rights movement in the United States. He later became a US congressman and a prominent voice for human rights and justice around the world. In the prologue to his memoir, Lewis tells a story from his childhood to describe his vision of how we can face profound challenges and make a better world.

[A]bout fifteen of us children were outside my aunt Seneva's house, playing in her dirt yard. The sky began clouding over, the wind started picking up, lightning flashed far off in the distance, and suddenly I wasn't thinking about playing anymore; I was terrified . . .

Aunt Seneva was the only adult around, and as the sky blackened and the wind grew stronger, she herded us all inside.

Her house was not the biggest place around, and it seemed even smaller with so many children squeezed inside. Small and surprisingly quiet. All of the shouting and laughter that had been going on earlier, outside, had stopped.

The wind was howling now, and the house was starting to shake. We were scared. Even Aunt Seneva was scared.

And then it got worse. Now the house was beginning to sway. The wood plank flooring beneath us began to bend. And then, a corner of the room started lifting up.

I couldn't believe what I was seeing. None of us could. This storm was actually pulling the house toward the sky. With us inside it.

That was when Aunt Seneva told us to clasp hands. Line up and hold hands, she said, and we did as we were told. Then she had us walk as a group toward the corner of the room that was rising. From the kitchen to the front of the house we walked, the wind screaming outside, sheets of rain beating on the tin roof. Then we walked back in the other direction, as another end of the house began to lift.

And so it went, back and forth, fifteen children walking with the wind, holding that trembling house down with the weight of our small bodies.

More than half a century has passed since that day, and it has struck me more than once over those many years that our society is not unlike the children in that house, rocked again and again by the winds of one storm or another, the walls around us seeming at times as if they might fly apart.

It seemed that way in the 1960s, at the height of the civil rights movement, when America itself felt as if it might burst at the seams—so much tension, so many storms. But the people of conscience never left the house. They never ran away. They stayed, they came together and they did the best they could, clasping hands and moving toward the corner of the house that was the weakest.

And then another corner would lift, and we would go there.

And eventually, inevitably, the storm would settle, and the house would still stand.

But we knew another storm would come, and we would have to do it all over again.

And we did.

And we still do, all of us. You and I.

Children holding hands, walking with the wind. . . .

Sample Reflection Questions

Use or adapt these questions to address your goals for student reflection and civic participation.

- What does choosing to participate mean to you? In what ways do you participate in the communities around you? How might you participate more deeply?

- How can our memory and understanding of history inspire and guide our choices in the world today?

- What role does history play in a healthy democracy? Is it necessary to acknowledge past injustices in order for democracy to be possible in the present?

- No matter where you live, your community has a history. What do you know or think you know about the history of your local community? Is some of your community's history unacknowledged or forgotten today? How might you discover and explore unacknowledged or forgotten histories of your community? How might awareness of the past change your understanding of the place where you live?

- Describe a time when you felt voiceless or powerless. What led you to feel that way?

- Describe a time when your voice was strong. What helped you find the "power in your gut" to express yourself?

- What can we do, alone and with others, to confront racism? How can we as individuals and as citizens make a positive difference in our school, community, nation, and world?

- Is bullying an accepted behavior in your school? Is being an upstander an accepted behavior? What steps can a community take to change its social norms (the behavior and language that a community considers acceptable)?

- Some people believe that artists should focus on beauty and avoid politics. Do you agree or disagree? Why? How can art promote human rights? What function can art have in political struggles? In education?

- In what ways can online activism influence social norms, or the beliefs and behavior that a community finds acceptable? How might online activism influence people's choices when they aren't online? What are the powers and limitations of online activism?

- How might the internet and social media affect the ways that people define "we" and "they"? In what ways might the internet and social media be useful in breaking down divisions in society? In what ways might these platforms be used to deepen or amplify those divisions?

- Former US President Barack Obama argues that we "cheat ourselves of progress" when we refuse to compromise. Do you agree or disagree? Why? How can we figure out when we can compromise to make progress? Are there any ideals or beliefs that should never be compromised?

- William Henry Hastie, the first African American to serve as a federal judge in the United States, said: "Democracy is a process, not a static condition. It is becoming rather than being. It can easily be lost, but never is fully won. Its essence is eternal struggle." What do you think Hastie meant? What else do you think is part of the "essence" of democracy?

- Which do you think is a more effective way to change a society: through laws or by influencing people's attitudes and beliefs? How might the two strategies work together?

- What is an example of a community that you belong to? What makes you feel part of that community?

- How can social media and the internet or digital technology help us help others in our communities and the world? When can social media or the internet be dangerous or destructive?

- According to writer Suzanne Goldsmith, having a common cause forms the true foundation of community. She writes,

> [C]ommunities are not built of friends, or of groups of people with similar styles and tastes, or even of people who like and understand each other. They are built of people who feel they are part of something that is bigger than themselves: a shared goal or enterprise. . . . To build a community requires only the ability to see value in others; to look at them and see a potential partner in one's enterprise.

What is the most valuable idea in the paragraph above? What makes you say that? Have you had an experience of connecting over a common cause in your own life and relationships?

- What factors can divide a community or break it apart? How can members of a community help it rebuild and become stronger?

- After studying the actions of rescuers during genocide, Ervin Staub wrote: "Goodness, like evil, often begins in small steps. Heroes evolve; they aren't born."

How do you define a hero? If goodness does indeed begin in small steps, what might that mean for the choices we make on a daily basis, even when we are not in the midst of a crisis?

Suggested Quotations for Reflection

"The great social justice changes in our country have happened when people came together, organized, and took direct action. It is this right that sustains and nurtures our democracy today. The civil rights movement, the labor movement, the women's movement, and the equality movement for our LGBT brothers and sisters are all manifestations of these rights."

—Dolores Huerta, American labor leader and civil rights activist

"If I cannot do great things, I can do small things in a great way."

—Martin Luther King Jr., minister and civil rights activist

"If you have come here to help me, you are wasting your time. But if you have come because your liberation is bound up with mine, then let us work together."

—Aboriginal activists group, Queensland, Australia, 1970s

"Inevitably, people ask me, 'What can I do?' What kind of question is that? Look around you. Once you identify what you want to do, don't ask for the masses to help you, because they won't come."

—Franklin McCain, civil rights movement activist

"I raise up my voice—not so I can shout but so that those without a voice can be heard . . . "

—Malala Yousafzai, Pakistani activist and Nobel Peace Prize winner

"Realize that you don't have to be extraordinary to change the world. You just have to do ordinary things on a constant basis. Stand up each day."

—Charles Mauldin, civil rights activist

"So long as we have enough people in this country willing to fight for their rights, we'll be called a democracy."

—Roger Nash Baldwin, co-founder of the American Civil Liberties Union

"Somebody has to stand when other people are sitting. Somebody has to speak when other people are quiet."

—Bryan Stevenson, social justice activist and founder of the Equal Justice Initiative

"Never doubt that a small group of thoughtful, committed citizens can change the world; indeed, it's the only thing that ever has."

—Margaret Mead, cultural anthropologist

"Sometimes change comes not in the first round, but at the second, third or fourth. Change starts with one person questioning, challenging, speaking up and doing something to make a difference. We can each make a difference . . . because each of us is already part of the community where racism exists and thrives."

—Paul Kivel, writer, educator, activist

"I swore never to be silent whenever and wherever human beings endure suffering and humiliation. We must always take sides. Neutrality helps the oppressor, never the victim."

—Elie Wiesel, writer, Holocaust survivor, Nobel Peace Prize winner

"You have to go through life with more than just passion for change; you need a strategy. . . . Not just awareness, but action."

—President Barack Obama

"You cannot, you cannot use someone else's fire. You can only use your own. And in order to do that, you must first be willing to believe that you have it."

—Audre Lorde, writer, feminist, civil rights activist

"If there's a book that you want to read, but it hasn't been written yet, then you must write it."

—Toni Morrison, writer

"It is not enough to be compassionate. You must act."

—His Holiness The Dalai Lama XIV

Choosing to Participate Readings

The readings included on the following pages provide examples of individuals and groups who have chosen to speak out or take action in order to make a positive difference in our world. These stories encourage students to think about ways we can participate as caring, thoughtful citizens in our lives today.

These examples can open students' eyes to the different ways of engaging and acting that are happening around them and to the tools that others have used to make positive changes in their own communities. Encountering these examples offers an opportunity for students to reflect on who they are, who they want to be, and what kind of world they want to help create. As students read these stories of upstanders, they might reflect on the following questions:

- What issue were they addressing? Why was it important to them?
- What were their goals, tools, and strategies?
- How did these individuals enlist allies and respond to success and failure?

You can also use these readings to perform "levers of power" analyses (see the handout on page 65). Additional CTP readings can be found in Chapter 12: Choosing to Participate of *Holocaust and Human Behavior*, available at facinghistory.org/ctp-links.

The Teaching Idea "Youth Taking Charge: Placing Student Activism in Historical Context," available at facinghistory.org/ctp-links, provides a number of resources on student activism, including related news articles. Another valuable resource, providing examples of students acting to create safe schools free from stereotypes, intolerance, and hate, is the Not in Our School streaming video collection found at NIOT.org/videos/nios.

Bullying at School

A bullying incident in school is often the first time a teenager is confronted with the decision of whether to be an upstander or a bystander. In a world full of injustice, suffering, and other social problems, the choice to participate can actually originate very close to home.

The following stories highlight the power of students to make positive change by taking seemingly small actions in response to bullying in their own school communities.

In Canada, two students responded this way when a classmate was taunted because of what he wore:

> Two Nova Scotia students are being praised across North America for the way they turned the tide against the bullies who picked on a fellow student for wearing pink.
>
> The victim — a Grade 9 boy at Central Kings Rural High School in the small community of Cambridge — wore a pink polo shirt on his first day of school.
>
> Bullies harassed the boy, called him a homosexual for wearing pink and threatened to beat him up, students said.
>
> Two Grade 12 students — David Shepherd and Travis Price — heard the news and decided to take action.
>
> "I just figured enough was enough," said Shepherd.
>
> They went to a nearby discount store and bought 50 pink shirts, including tank tops, to wear to school the next day.
>
> Then the two went online to email classmates to get them on board with their anti-bullying cause that they dubbed a "sea of pink."
>
> But a tsunami of support poured in the next day.
>
> Not only were dozens of students outfitted with the discount tees, but hundreds of students showed up wearing their own pink clothes, some head-to-toe.
>
> When the bullied student, who has never been identified, walked into school to see his fellow students decked out in pink, some of his classmates said it was a powerful moment. He may have even blushed a little.
>
> "Definitely it looked like there was a big weight lifted off his shoulders. He went from looking right depressed to being as happy as can be," said Shepherd.
>
> And there's been nary a peep from the bullies since, which Shepherd says just goes to show what a little activism will do.

"If you can get more people against them . . . to show that we're not going to put up with it and support each other, then they're not as big as a group as they think they are," he says.[1]

At Orange High School in Pepper Pike, Ohio, students responded in a different way when they witnessed bullying in their school. They began by trying to learn more about where bullying was happening. After surveying classmates about where they had witnessed bullying, students created maps that showed where bullying incidents commonly took place. "Bully hotspots" included the cafeteria, media lab, and locker rooms.

Explaining the motivation for the project, one student said, "We wanted to spread awareness because people need to know what bullying is. People need to know that it exists in our school. I think addressing it and defining it and spreading awareness that it exists is the first step in preventing and combating it."[2]

Because some of the acts of bullying had been rather subtle, some students either did not recognize them or felt unsure about naming them as bullying. To address this problem, student leaders created a "flash freeze" demonstration to dramatize what bullying looks like so that other students could recognize it and call it out more easily. The demonstration showed students frozen in mid-action, portraying an incident of bullying. Other students in the demonstration would then name the actions, using words like *physical*, *verbal*, *exclusion*, and *cyber-bullying*. The map of bullying "hotspots" and the demonstrations opened up a larger conversation about how to create a safer school and made it more difficult for some students to ignore bullying when they saw it happening.

One student talked about how the project affected his future choices:

> I got made fun of for my name because it didn't sound American, so I was really quiet. I never really talked in school 'cause I was scared of being made fun of. And when you don't talk, you don't make friends. It's a chain reaction. It just gets worse and worse. You lose your confidence. You don't want to speak to anyone. So, I guess doing this project really helps. Whenever I see someone getting bullied, I step in. No matter what age they are, if I know them or not, it doesn't matter. Because I just think about how much I would have loved for someone to step in when I was getting bullied.[3]

1 "Bullied student tickled pink by schoolmates' T-shirt campaign," CBC News Canada, last modified September 18, 2007, accessed July 12, 2016.
2 Transcribed from "Students Map Bully Zones to Create a Safer School" (video), *Not in Our Town* website, accessed July 12, 2016.
3 Ibid.

 FACING HISTORY AND OURSELVES   www.facinghistory.org

Student Activism: From the Civil Rights Movement to Parkland Today

On March 7, 1965, 17-year-old Charles Mauldin took his place near the front of a line of marchers heading out of Selma, Alabama, with a demand for equal voting rights. The peaceful marchers were brutally assaulted by local law enforcement; Mauldin was so close to John Lewis that he still remembers the sound of an officer's billy club cracking Lewis's skull. The drama of the Selma-to-Montgomery march transfixed Americans and was a pivotal moment in the struggle for civil rights. Over 50 years later, as student activists were drawing national attention with their calls for reform in the wake of the Parkland school shooting in 2018, Mauldin reflected on the power of young people to spark social change and offered insights for today's emerging activists.

How did you get involved with the civil rights movement? What got you started as an activist?

I didn't start off as an activist. I started off as an observer of little incidents that came into my life from being in a segregated environment. We were taught to call older people "Mr." and "Mrs." but I saw white people half or one-third the age of my mother and father calling them by their first names, and they didn't say "yes sir" or "no sir." Little things like that grated on me. And then Bernard Lafayette came to town in 1963 and he began to ask simple questions: "Why can't your parents vote?" Or, "Why can't you drink out of the white water fountain? Why can't you use the bathrooms in the stores downtown?" Little questions like that left me puzzled. I had no answer. We'd been brought up in an environment where we didn't think outside of the box because it was too dangerous. It was the job of the state, the county, and the local police department to basically keep us contained.

But Bernard Lafayette sort of piqued our curiosity, and we realized that anybody in my community who was black had one form of indignity or another heaped upon them—each different, but we all shared being discriminated against and suffered indignities day in and day out. When I got in the movement, I began to realize the political and the human solution to our situation was through non-violence. And once I recognized that, I became involved in marches and demonstrations. I became the head of the Lowndes County Youth League in mid-1964, and, from that point, we marched almost every day until later in 1965, culminating in the march to Montgomery. I hardly spent any time in school in all of 1965. We basically took the year off to be involved in demonstrations. I started off at 16 and was 17 during the march to Montgomery.

How did it matter that young people were at the forefront?

It made an impact in almost every major movement. It was young people in Montgomery who helped to win the Montgomery Bus Boycott. Young people in Birmingham who provided the leadership in the Birmingham movement. It was the young people in Selma who sustained the movement until the adults showed up. Young people in South Africa who helped with the liberation there. Young people are always a fire that causes change.

I think it's because they don't have the disadvantage of being overexposed to what the consequences of their actions could be. They respond more innocently to the issues at hand, and they don't have the restraints on them that adults have, like paying bills or losing jobs. Just as in Florida right now, they are responding passionately to an issue they see that is vital to them, and the response is simply open honesty.

How do you stay persistent when progress is slow to come?

When a movement gets created, it's because there's something inherent in how people respond. They're not responding to circumstances outside of themselves, they're responding to a circumstance that involves them, and they have a personal commitment and a personal involvement, so it's real to them. It's not external, it's internal, and that's what I think motivates them. That's what was true for us. The issue [of school violence] is not going to go away, and it's in the fabric of [the Parkland students'] lives now. And I think that's a self-sustaining type of situation.

What do you want today's young activists to know? What advice do you have for them?

You have to take one step at a time, day by day. John Lewis once said, "Find ways to get in the way of what is wrong in life." Injustice, discrimination, racism, and now gun violence. Find ways to get in the way of what you see as wrong. And realize that you don't have to be extraordinary to change the world. You just have to do ordinary things on a constant basis. Stand up each day.[1]

1   Charles Mauldin, interview by Laura Tavares (Facing History and Ourselves), "Student Activism: From the Civil Rights Movement to Parkland Today," *Facing Today* (blog), March 7, 2018, https://facingtoday.facinghistory.org/student-activism-from-the-civil-rights-movement-to-parkland-today.

 FACING HISTORY AND OURSELVES   www.facinghistory.org

How a Jewish Civil Rights Activist Taught Me to Fight for All Rights

High school student Julia Clardy wrote this piece as part of the Rising Voices Fellowship, a program of the Jewish Women's Archive (JWA). It was originally published on JWA's blog, *Jewish Women, Amplified.*

In the summer of 1963, Miriam Cohen Glickman was arrested in Albany, Georgia, along with several other Civil Rights activists. While in jail, they went on a week-long hunger strike as a form of protest. This passionate solidarity with those seeking civil rights was a large part of Miriam's career as an activist.

Miriam grew up in Indianapolis and came from a relatively wealthy Jewish family. Her high school experience is described in depth in *Going South: Jewish Women in the Civil Rights Movement* by Debra L. Schultz. In regard to forming relationships with African American students in her school, Miriam is quoted as saying: "Jewish kids were more comfortable than a lot of the other white kids being friends with the black kids." Miriam goes on to describe a sort of shared black and Jewish experience, in the sense that black and Jewish kids were not seen as "all-American" high schoolers like their white Christian counterparts.

Discrimination towards minorities is not at all new, but what I find inspiring about Miriam is her passion for demanding better treatment, not just for Jews, but for other marginalized groups as well. In Miriam's career as an activist, she played major roles in the Civil Rights Movement, and utilized her father's platform as the editor of the *National Jewish Post and Opinion* to spread the word about the arrests and mistreatment of civil rights activists.

It's common to feel helpless in times when racial injustice, while always present, is particularly prevalent. Police brutality towards black and brown people in the United States is impossible to ignore. As a white person, I feel it is my responsibility to use my platform to elevate the voices of others, and make sure their struggles and stories are heard. Miriam's story can help us navigate this difficult reality by teaching us that in order to achieve justice for ourselves, we must fight for the freedom of others as well. At times when Jewish people have been targeted, we have too often faced silence from those with the power to help. Therefore, as Jews, we cannot stay silent when others are targeted. We know where that leads.

To me, Miriam Cohen Glickman's story is the epitome of what it means to be a Jewish activist. As a young Jewish woman who's passionate about racial justice in America, I believe it's imperative that we as Jews not only look out for ourselves, but for other minorities as well. My grandmother and I attend a Black Lives Matter vigil once a month together, and this October, the vigil fell close to Sukkot. Upon arriving at the meeting place, I saw dozens of people chatting and picking out signs to hold during the vigil. Among the people in the crowd were the Rabbi that lives on my grandmother's street and his wife. Even though I'm sure he had a lot to do leading up to Sukkot, he still made it a priority to devote his night to fighting for others. Being in this environment with other Jews feels incredibly powerful, and I know the Rabbi and I share the sentiment that we must show up for oppressed minorities. It's not enough to fight for causes that only benefit your community. The fight for justice is universal, and I am proud that my Jewish education has taught me to embrace that ideal.[1]

1   Julia Clardy, "Solidarity Sister," *Jewish Women, Amplified* (blog), November 29, 2017, jwa.org/blog/risingvoices/solidarity-sister. Also published on "How a Jewish Civil Rights Activist Taught Me to Fight for All Rights," *Facing Today* (blog), https://facingtoday.facinghistory.org/how-a-jewish-civil-rights-activist-taught-me-to-fight-for-all-rights. Reproduced by permission of Julia Clardy.

The Voices of Millions

After internet use became widespread in the 1990s, anyone who could go online gained a new set of tools for sharing information, speaking out, and organizing responses to crises and problems that included natural disasters and mass violence. Today, millions of people use social media to express their opinions about issues in their local, national, and global communities. But although the internet has made civic participation easier, some people wonder whether online activism really makes a difference.

On March 25, 2013, the Human Rights Campaign (HRC)—an organization that supports lesbian, gay, bisexual, and transgender rights—urged people to change their Facebook profile pictures to a pink-on-red equals sign to show support for marriage equality. That week, the Supreme Court of the United States was debating a case that involved gay marriage. One day later, hundreds of thousands of people had changed their profile pictures to the HRC symbol.

There is little evidence that the HRC Facebook campaign had any effect on the deliberations of the Supreme Court justices. And critics of the campaign worried that too many of those who changed their profile pictures felt satisfied that by taking this relatively easy action, they had "done their part" to support marriage equality. Some critics of online activism have coined terms like "hashtag activism" and "slacktivism" to describe efforts such as the HRC profile-picture campaign that require little real participation. Scott Gilmore, a former Canadian diplomat, writes:

> A slacktivist is someone who believes it is more important to be seen to help than to actually help. He will wear a T-shirt to raise awareness. She will wear a wristband to demonstrate support, sign a petition to add her voice, share a video to spread the message, even pour a bucket of ice over her head. The one thing slacktivists don't do is help by, for example, giving money or time to those who are truly making the world a better place . . . [1]

Many experts disagree with the skeptics. They argue that the collective voices of groups of internet users can make a real difference. Discussing the HRC campaign, Matt Stempeck, a researcher at the MIT Center for Civic Media, writes:

> No one taking these actions is expecting a direct response from the Supreme Court. . . . Yet this action, taken by many, can matter. We know that support for gay marriage is linked with how likely it is we know someone who is openly gay. And we know that people care deeply about societal norms [social standards]. Ever-increasing support for gay equality, generated at the interpersonal level, is only strengthened by a mass outpouring of support on social networks. . . . By going pink, people are standing up as allies and creating the perception of a safe space within their own friendship communities online—spaces where gay people may face stigmas and bullying.[2]

1   Scott Gilmore, "The problem with #slacktivism," *Maclean's*, last modified November 11, 2014, accessed September 2, 2015.
2   J. Nathan Matias, Matt Stempeck, and Molly Sauter, "Green vs. Pink: Change Your Picture, Change the World," MIT Center for Civic Media, blog entry, posted March 28, 2013, accessed July 26, 2016.

In 2014, another online campaign suggested that the collective voice of a group of social media users can influence not just individual attitudes but also the behavior of institutions, such as the print and broadcast media. After an African American teenager was shot to death by a police officer in Ferguson, Missouri, in summer 2014, thousands of people used Twitter to protest the photograph of the teenager, taken from his Facebook page, that was published by many television networks, newspapers, and websites. Journalist James Poniewozik analyzed the online protest:

> The injury, a deadly one, came first. Unarmed 18-year-old Michael Brown was shot to death by police in Ferguson, Mo. Then came the insult: many news accounts used a photo of Brown that showed him, unsmiling, gesturing at the camera in a way that led to unsubstantiated claims that he was "flashing gang signs."
>
> This portrayal of Brown, who is African American, recalled the quasi-trial-by-photo of Trayvon Martin, another young black man shot to death. It became another racially charged statement in a controversial killing, as outlets illustrated their stories with pictures that—rather than show the dead teen smiling or in a family context—led commenters to call him a "thug" and thus to suggest that he brought his death on himself.
>
> So as people protested in the streets of Ferguson, a meta-protest began on social media. Twitter users, especially African Americans, began a meta-protest, posting pairs of photos with the hashtag #IfTheyGunnedMeDown: a young man in a military dress uniform, say, and the same poster flipping off the camera. If I got shot down, each post asked, which version of me would the media show you?
>
> The term "hashtag activism" has become a kind of putdown lately, with the connotation that it's substituting gestures for action, as if getting something trending is a substitute for actually going out and engaging with the world . . .
>
> But #IfTheyGunnedMeDown was a simple, ingenious DIY [do-it-yourself] form of media criticism: direct, powerful, and meaningful on many levels. It made the blunt point that every time a media outlet chooses a picture of someone like Brown, it makes a statement. It created identification: so many ordinary people—students, servicemen and women, community volunteers—could be made to look like a public menace with one photo dropped in a particular context. And it made a particular racial point: that it's so much easier, given our culture's racial baggage, for a teenager of color to be made to look like a "thug" than [a] white teen showing off for a camera the exact same way.
>
> It was a brilliant media critique, and while Twitter and other platforms may have no magical power to stop shootings or catch warlords, one thing they are very good at is catching the attention of the media. Journalists pay attention to Twitter—disproportionate attention, maybe—and that makes it a very, very good place to deliver the modern version of a letter to the editor . . .
>
> #IfTheyGunnedMeDown is not going to stop anyone from being gunned down, but it most likely lodged in the memory of editors and producers who make judgments every day. Sure, many of them are already aware of the power of

FACING HISTORY AND OURSELVES   www.facinghistory.org

image choices, but #IfTheyGunnedMeDown chose its own images to make a powerful statement—one that people are likely to remember the next time "if" becomes "when."[3]

3   James Poniewozik, "#IfTheyGunnedMeDown and What Hashtag Activism Does Right," *TIME* online, last modified August 11, 2014, accessed September 2, 2015.

Brother Outsider: Remembering Gay Civil Rights Leader Bayard Rustin

LGBTQ Pride Month every June is an opportunity to explore and amplify the stories of LGBTQ people past and present. But even during Pride Month, we seldom hear stories of LGBTQ people of color. Described as the "unknown hero" of the civil rights movement, Bayard Rustin was the openly gay African American civil rights activist who served as the chief organizer of the historic March on Washington. But why is Rustin so often omitted from the pantheon of African American leaders we learn about in school and pop culture—and how can including his story enrich our understanding of black and LGBTQ history?

After exploring an array of activist circles in his early years, Rustin worked as a political organizer with the Fellowship of Reconciliation—work that led him to his mentor, legendary labor leader A. Philip Randolph. And this mentorship would thrust Rustin into the center of major debates about who could represent the civil rights movement and why. Convinced that Rustin's acumen as an organizer could advance the movement, Randolph successfully urged Rustin to meet with Dr. Martin Luther King Jr. and lend support to the Montgomery Bus Boycott. Though Rustin did most of his work behind the scenes, he played a crucial role in helping King adopt a nonviolent philosophy while serving as his special assistant, ghostwriter, and movement strategist.

Though King had read Mahatma Gandhi's writings, "it was Bayard Rustin, and a few other pacifists," says scholar Michael G. Long, "who really encouraged Dr. King to accept pacifism as a way of life." As he became central to King's inner circle, Rustin would have a defining impact on the vision and strategy of the civil rights movement, championing nonviolent direct action as the most effective means of disrupting racism and violence. But for all of his influence, including his work with the historic Southern Christian Leadership Conference (SCLC), Rustin remained out of the spotlight and was never permitted to become a highly visible "face" of the movement due to his sexual orientation and former political affiliations.

Rustin's marginality within the movement reached new heights in 1960 when a powerful opponent targeted his sexual orientation to gain the upper hand over the SCLC. King, Rustin, and Randolph had planned a protest outside of the Democratic National Convention (DNC) that year to challenge the party's position on civil rights. DNC leadership then asked black congressman Adam Clayton Powell to stop the march, at which point he threatened to leak a fabricated news story to the press alleging an affair between King and Rustin. King subsequently distanced himself from Rustin, leading Rustin to resign from the SCLC.

FACING HISTORY AND OURSELVES   www.facinghistory.org

Despite the pain of betrayal that Rustin faced during this chapter, his activism continued, and he would re-enter the fold when King sought to deploy Rustin's talents once again. Determined to make his next endeavor a success, King brought Rustin on as the chief organizer of the March on Washington—one of the largest protests in US history, where King delivered his iconic "I Have a Dream" speech. Though King and his collaborators knew that they needed Rustin's unmatched skill, Rustin was kept out of the limelight again.

Though Rustin understood the strategic concerns that led peers to marginalize him within the movement, he recalled later in life that being his whole self in public remained vital throughout his life of activism. "It was an absolute necessity for me to declare homosexuality, because if I didn't . . . I was aiding and abetting the prejudice that was part of the effort to destroy me," Rustin said in an interview released on the *Making Gay History* podcast. And as the gay rights movement gained momentum in the 1980s, Rustin became a vocal figure.

Though Rustin's spirit of resistance had an unquestionable impact, many of the pressures that he faced remain decades later. As an openly gay black activist, Rustin was a political liability—a physical manifestation of an inconvenient truth about the civil rights movement: that the group of people whose rights needed to be defended was not merely comprised of straight black men. And yet, the leaders of the movement—shaped by their own prejudices and the desire to gain acceptance from the wider society—were prepared to jettison Rustin, other LGBTQ people, and women to advance the political vision they deemed legitimate and pragmatic.

This is the nature of respectability politics, or what happens when the experiences of some of a marginalized group's members (e.g., black LGBTQ people) are hushed or simply erased in the pursuit of progress. Leaders' attempts to control who could become the face of their movement were central political strategies, but we must ask who is left behind when these maneuvers limit who is able to speak and the stories we feel we can tell about our own histories.

In Rustin, we find the story of an openly gay black man who devoted his career to social change work and exhibited an abiding pride in who he was, even as he faced immense discrimination within and beyond his own communities. We also find a figure who—despite the betrayals and other challenges he faced—remained committed to civic engagement and the long game of promoting social change.[1]

---

1   Kaitlin Smith (Facing History and Ourselves), "Brother Outsider: Remembering Gay Civil Rights Leader Bayard Rustin," *Facing Today* (blog), June 17, 2019, https://facingtoday.facinghistory.org/brother-outsider-remembering-gay-civil-rights-leader-bayard-rustin.

Brainstorming Strategies

These strategies can be used to brainstorm small-group and class projects and expand student self-reflection by engaging in dialogue with a community of learners.

- **Graffiti Board:** Brainstorm project ideas on a graffiti board. Don't edit ideas at this point. Think big. Think small. Encourage creativity. Then discuss the results as a group. Invite students to share their visions for projects and desired outcomes.

- **Sticky Blast:** Give each student a stack of sticky notes and explain that they will spend ten minutes brainstorming ideas for a project that addresses the guiding question. Encourage them to think creatively and not edit their ideas. Tell them to write one idea per sticky note.

  - Then have students post their notes on the board, and, as a group, read them out loud, asking students to explain their ideas in two sentences or less. Then have them start to group their ideas into categories that they create. Once they have finished, see if there is a category that they want to use as a starting place to develop a final project.

  - Alternatively, you might create a web or map from the sticky notes. Write "class project" in the center of the piece of chart paper, and then start to create groupings of notes. Draw lines between notes and groupings, write connections and questions over the lines, and draw images to represent new ideas.

- **Idea Pass-Around:** Sit in a circle and give each student a piece of lined paper. Have them write a guiding question at the top, and then have them explain one or more project ideas. Remind them that they don't need to edit their ideas. Then have them pass their papers to the right. They should read the new paper and write any ideas that their peer's paper generates for them. They might expand on an idea, pose a question, or draw an image or map. Keep passing and writing until everyone has their original paper. Students should read their peers' comments and questions and then share new insights with the group.

- **Calling on a Hero:** Sit in a circle and have students respond to the following prompt in their journals: *Who is your hero or alter ego?* (Real people, past or present, or fictional characters from books, films, and comics are all fair game.) *What would your hero or alter ego do to make a positive impact on your school community?* Have students share their ideas in pairs or trios and then discuss what they can learn from how their heroes or alter egos would take on this project.

- **Storyboard:** After the group has generated some project ideas, have them work in teams of three or four to choose one idea and create a storyboard on the template, chart paper, or a long piece of butcher paper that uses images and text to explain the steps involved in carrying out the project. Groups can present their storyboards to the class, who might vote for one to implement or combine multiple ideas into a single project.

Culminating Reflection Routines

Use one of these reflection routines at the end of a Choosing to Participate project to reinforce students' learning and help them commit to continuing to participate.

Someday/Monday

Progress toward justice and equality does not always advance steadily. Great leaps forward are often met with backlash and disappointing steps backward. This strategy helps remind students of the importance of small steps, particularly when they are feeling overwhelmed by an issue.

- *Someday* I'm going to look for a way to . . . , but *Monday* I might choose to . . .

I Used to Think/Now I Think

This strategy can be used iteratively throughout student projects, as they research an issue and begin developing an action plan and again as a culminating reflection designed to highlight the importance of continuous learning and persistence.

- I came to this project thinking . . .
- Now I think . . .
- So next I'll try . . .

Start, Stop, Continue

This prompt can be used as a culminating reflection designed to reinforce both students' learning and any shifts in mindset they experienced.

Because of what I have learned and thought about during this process, I will:

- Start . . .
- Stop . . .
- Continue . . .

FROM REFLECTION TO ACTION: A CHOOSING TO PARTICIPATE TOOLKIT

Action

Public Memory and the Role of Memorials

Essential Questions

- What is the purpose of memorials and monuments? What impact do they have on us and the way we think about history?

- What can we learn from memorials and monuments about the beliefs and values of the people who created them?

- How can individuals and communities shape public memory and influence people's beliefs and attitudes through the creation of memorials and monuments?

Materials

IMAGE GALLERY
Introducing Memorials and Monuments

READING
Acknowledging the Past to Shape the Present

READING
Creating a New Narrative

Teaching Strategies

(see facinghistory.org/ctp-links)
Chunking
Annotating and Paraphrasing
Gallery Walk

Learning Objectives

- Students will understand that monuments represent one way that communities and individuals both remember and celebrate the past as well as shape future generations' understanding of history.

- Students will understand that when creating monuments, artists and communities make choices about what aspects of a particular history are worth remembering and what parts are intentionally left out.

- Students will understand the connection between history and democracy and how taking an active role in the commemoration of public space can be an act of civic participation.

Overview

Events in August 2017 in Charlottesville, Virginia, where white supremacists protesting the removal of a Confederate monument incited violence that led to the death of a counter-protester, raised important issues about history, public memory, and the symbolism of public space.

This lesson is designed to help students understand the role that memorials and monuments play in expressing a society's values and shaping its memory of the past. The lesson invites students to explore how public monuments and memorials serve as a selective lens on the past that, in turn, powerfully shapes our understanding of the present. It also explores how new public symbols might be created to tell a countervailing narrative that seeks to change or correct the previous, dominant understanding of history.

In Memphis, Tennessee, high school students and activists undertook such a project when they began to reckon with the forgotten history of lynching in their community. In this lesson, students will connect these efforts to the idea of participatory democracy, analyzing how the creation of new historical symbols can be understood as an effort to transform communities and shape collective memory. In the final activity, students will choose to participate by becoming public historians themselves. They will design their own memorial to represent a historical idea, event, or person they deem worthy of commemoration.

Context

Monuments and memorials serve multiple functions in the communities in which they are erected. When the members of a community create a monument or memorial, they are making a statement about the ideas, values, or individuals they think their society should remember, if not honor. As a result, these structures not only influence the way people understand the subjects of their commemoration, but they also reveal the beliefs of the people and the time period in which they were created. They thus serve as historical artifacts in themselves.

While some memorials are spontaneous, such as flowers left on the roadside after a car accident, most are carefully designed and intended for permanence. The process can involve an entire community raising funds, forming committees, and selecting designers, sculptors, or architects. These structures can be a response to loss and death, as is often the case with memorials, or they can be celebratory in nature, as is typical of monuments. (Note: While some see value in making a distinction between the terms *memorial* and *monument* for the reasons listed above, there are so many exceptions to these rules that this lesson will use the terms interchangeably.)

Memorials and monuments are designed to convey forceful messages about the events or individuals they commemorate. Each has embedded in it a particular perspective, an interpretation, and a set of values or judgments. As a result, these public structures often raise contentious questions:

- Why are some historical events or individuals deemed worthy of public commemoration, while others are not? How does that sorting take place?

- If these structures cannot tell the whole story, what part of the story, and whose story, do they tell? What points of view should be left out? Who decides?

- Who do we entrust to interpret the past for present and future generations?

The debates over these questions often reflect existing and longstanding divisions within a society. Therefore, the process of creating—or removing—monuments and memorials can be a battleground where competing perceptions and profoundly different memories struggle to control the interpretation of history.

Activities

1. Introduce Memorials and Monuments

Before engaging more directly with memorials and monuments, introduce and define their purpose more generally, using some examples with which students are already familiar.

- Begin brainstorming with students some of the purposes of memorials and monuments. What purpose do they serve? Who creates them? Why?

- Then break the class into pairs and ask them to view the Introducing Memorials and Monuments image gallery and choose a memorial or monument to study. In their journals, ask them to describe the memorial or monument they selected. They might also sketch it or tape a photograph into their journals. Their description should answer the following basic questions: What is it? What does it look like? Where is it, and what is around it? What is it about this memorial that prompted you to choose it to analyze? You might permit students to do some brief internet research to find some of these details that are not visible in the images in the gallery.

- Then ask the pairs to discuss these questions:
  - Who is the intended audience for the memorial?
  - What, specifically, is the memorial representing or commemorating?
  - What story or message do you think the artist was trying to convey to the intended audience? What might the memorial be leaving out?
  - How does the memorial convey its intended story or message? What materials did the artist use? What experience did the artist create for the audience?

- Lead a brief class discussion in which students share some of their examples, and then focus on the following questions:
  - Why might people want to build memorials? List as many reasons as the class can brainstorm.
  - How might one's identity affect how one understands and commemorates history?
  - What are the consequences of remembering a history? What are the consequences of forgetting a history?

2. Read about Efforts to Transform Historical Symbols

In 2013, Bryan Stevenson, a lawyer who started the Equal Justice Initiative to challenge bias and inequity in the US justice system, launched a campaign to memorialize historical sites of racist violence across the American South. He began leading a project to identify, record, and mark the places where lynchings occurred, both to accurately report the number of people killed and to teach the public about the roots of twenty-first-century racial injustice.

Individual communities have also looked for opportunities to recognize and reckon with incidents of racist violence that took place in their midst. In small groups, have students read the text "Acknowledging the Past to Shape the Present" and the speech "Creating a New Narrative." (Depending on students' reading level, you may want to use the Chunking or Annotating and Paraphrasing strategies.) Then ask students to answer the following questions in their journals:

- Why do you think that the Overton High School students were shocked to learn that Ell Persons's lynching happened so close to their school, in an area that was familiar to them?

- How do students and activists intend to commemorate Persons's lynching? What do they hope their efforts will achieve?

- In her speech, how does Marti Tippens Murphy define the terms *upstander* and *bystander*? Why does she believe that the Overton High School students are upstanders?

Next, have students discuss the following questions, first in their small groups and then as a class:

- How can acknowledging and memorializing a troubling moment in history be an act of civic participation? How can it be an act of hope?

- What role does history play in a healthy democracy? Is it necessary to acknowledge past injustices in order to achieve a more just and equitable society?

- No matter where you live, your community has a history. Is any part of your community's history unacknowledged or forgotten today? How might you discover and explore such histories? Could awareness of the past change your understanding of the place you call home?

3. **Create Your Own Memorial**

Now ask students to design or write their own memorials.

- Ask students to choose a historical idea, event, or individual in their local community, school, or family that they would want to memorialize. You could also focus on ideas, events, and individuals specifically related to your current unit of study. It may be necessary to give students some time or suggested resources to research the ideas, events, or individuals that they are considering.

- Before they begin, ask students to respond to the following prompts in their journals:
  - What historical idea, individual, or event is most important for you and others to remember? Why?
  - What message do you want the memorial to convey? How does this message augment or challenge what others are likely to know about the historical idea, event, or individual?
  - Who is the audience for the memorial?
  - How will the memorial communicate your ideas? What specific materials, shapes, imagery, or words will it include?

- Once they have thought through these questions, ask students to create something. It can be as simple as a sketch or as complex as a model made with physical materials.

- Instruct students to title their memorial and write a brief description, or artist's statement, to accompany it. In their statement, students should explain their rationale for choosing this particular place, event, or individual. How might their memorial change perspectives on the subject?

- Once the memorials or paragraphs are complete, use the Gallery Walk strategy to arrange them so that students can observe and analyze each other's work.

- Debrief the Gallery Walk as a class. Discuss the following questions with students:

  - What did you notice about your classmates' memorials?

  - What patterns emerged?

  - What new perspectives did you gain about a historical idea, individual, or event, or about the process of recording and remembering history?

Note: You may need to modify or adapt these guidelines to take into account the materials you have on hand for students to use in building their memorials. Some teachers encourage students to use modeling clay, construction paper, or similar materials for their memorials, while others simply instruct students to create a sketch or diagram of the memorial without building it. Even if your students don't create a physical representation, you can ask them to write the paragraph-length artist's statement described above to explain their ideas.

Extension

1. Elevate Other Voices and Histories

Studying and creating memorials is one way to apply the lessons of history to the present. Another way students can choose to participate is through critically reviewing the stories and experiences included in their studies. The essential question for such a CTP project could be: *What is the narrative of history that we need in order to promote a more just and equitable society? Whose voices need to be included or amplified?*

After reflecting on and researching whose voices or narratives have been included, left out, and why, students can consider different ways to elevate the missing narrative or voices, including:

- Teaching others through a student-led community teach-in

- Telling personal stories through an exhibit, website, or podcast

- Advocating to change the name of a school, team, or public building

- Writing a letter to the textbook company

- Writing and publishing additions to the unit for future classes

Similarly, students in an ELA classroom can do an audit of the ELA curriculum to see which perspectives and voices are not being represented and make a recommendation to their administration or the district for new titles to be added.

Introducing Memorials and Monuments

David L. Moore - US NE / Alamy Stock Photo

FDNY Memorial Wall

DEDICATED TO THOSE WHO FELL AND TO THOSE WHO CARRY ON

This memorial commemorates the New York City firefighters who lost their lives on September 11, 2001.

Lincoln Memorial

The Lincoln Memorial, which overlooks the National Mall in Washington, D.C., honors the life and death of the 16th US president.

FACING
HISTORY
AND
OURSELVES

www.facinghistory.org

Vietnam Veterans Memorial

This memorial in Washington, D.C., displays the names of Americans who fought and died in the Vietnam War.

Stolpersteine

Stolpersteine (stumbling stones) in Sušice, Czech Republic, mark the site where the four members of the Gutmann family lived before they were murdered in the Holocaust.

Acknowledging the Past to Shape the Present

How we think about the past can play a powerful role in shaping the present. In 2013, Bryan Stevenson, a lawyer who started the Equal Justice Initiative to challenge bias and inequity in the US justice system, launched a campaign to memorialize historical sites of racist violence across the American South. He began leading a project to identify, record, and mark the places where lynchings occurred, both to accurately report the number of people killed and to teach the public about the roots of twenty-first-century racial injustice. Between 1877 and 1950, at least 3,950 African Americans were lynched (executed by a mob, without a trial, usually by hanging) after being accused of "crimes" such as knocking on a white woman's door, wearing an army uniform in public after World War II, or bumping into a white girl while running for a train.

Often, Stevenson says, the hangings became public carnivals designed to instill fear. He calls them incidents of domestic terrorism, purposefully used to enforce racial subordination and segregation.[1] "We cannot heal the deep wounds inflicted during the era of racial terrorism until we tell the truth about it," writes Stevenson. "The geographic, political, economic, and social consequences of decades of terror lynchings can still be seen in many communities today and the damage created by lynching needs to be confronted and discussed. Only then can we meaningfully address the contemporary problems that are lynching's legacy."[2]

Students at Overton High School in Memphis, Tennessee, came to a similar conclusion in 2016 after learning about the lynching of Ell Persons. Zoey Parker, a senior, encountered the Persons case while doing a research assignment and shared the story with her classmates. Persons was an African American woodcutter who was burned alive in 1917 after being accused of murder. About 5,000 people from the Memphis community came to watch the event, which was prominently covered by the local newspaper, and gruesome postcards were made showing photos of his head. His murderers had decapitated his body after they had burned him to death.

When Parker's teacher, Dr. Marilyn Taylor, informed her students that the lynching had occurred close to their school, near a present-day drive-in movie theater, students were stunned that something so brutal could have taken place in their own backyard. They were also shocked to realize that an incident that had been widely known about when it happened was almost completely lost to memory a century later. Dr. Taylor reflected, "They have all been to this drive-in. They had a multitude of questions the following day so we put our scheduled lesson aside and they began their investigation."[3]

1   John M. Glionna, "Civil rights lawyer seeks to commemorate another side of Southern heritage: Lynchings," *Los Angeles Times*, July 5, 2015, accessed July 13, 2016, https://www.latimes.com/nation/la-na-alabama-lynchings-20150705-story.html.

2   "Lynching in America: Confronting the Legacy of Racial Terror," Equal Justice Initiative, accessed July 13, 2016, http://eji.org/reports/lynching-in-america.

3   Quoted in Marti Tippens Murphy, "Students Memorialize a Past Tragedy to Create a More Hopeful Future," *Facing Today* (blog), entry posted May 23, 2016, accessed July 13, 2016. http://facingtoday.facinghistory.org/students-memorialize-a-past-tragedy-to-create-a-more-hopeful-future.

The students felt they needed to do more than investigate the history, so Dr. Taylor asked them, "What are we going to do about it?"[4]

They decided to turn research into action and form a nonprofit organization called Students Uniting Memphis. This group launched a project to create a memorial garden at the site of Ell Persons's lynching, which in 2016 contained an abandoned bridge support surrounded by river overflow and dense foliage. Students also began to educate their community about Ell Persons. They reached out to a nearby high school where, in 1917, students had been released from classes to attend Persons's lynching, and they partnered with another nonprofit, The Lynching Sites Project of Memphis, which was formed after its founders heard Bryan Stevenson speak about the importance of facing the past.

In 2016, 99 years after Persons's death, more than 100 people gathered at the site of his lynching for an interfaith prayer service. The Lynching Sites Project, Students Uniting Memphis, the Memphis chapter of the NAACP—which was formed in 1917 in response to the Persons lynching—and other student groups then began working together to involve 5,000 people in a commemoration of the 100th anniversary of the lynching in 2017. Students from a Facing History and Ourselves student leadership group based in Memphis were among those who became involved.

"Young people today have to take action in order for history not to repeat itself," said Zoey Parker, the student who first researched Persons's case for Dr. Taylor's class. "We have to be mindful enough to understand we cannot continue to make the same mistakes as those before us."[5]

Connection Questions

1. Why do you think that the Overton High School students were shocked to learn that Ell Persons's lynching happened so close to their school, in an area that was familiar to them?

2. How do students and activists intend to commemorate Persons's lynching? What do they hope their efforts will achieve?

3. How can making a disturbing moment in history visible be an act of civic participation? How can it be an act of hope?

4. What role does history play in a healthy democracy? Is it necessary to acknowledge past injustices in order for democracy to be possible in the present?

5. No matter where you live, your community has a history. Is some of your community's history unacknowledged or forgotten today? How might you discover and explore such histories? Could awareness of the past change your understanding of the place you call home?

4 Ibid.
5 Ibid.

www.facinghistory.org

Creating a New Narrative

Marti Tippens Murphy is the executive director of the Facing History and Ourselves Memphis office. She delivered this speech at the dedication of the Lynching of Ell Persons Historical Marker on May 21, 2017.

We've all heard that history shapes the present, that it isn't even past. You could say history is our inheritance, that history is us.

We are the heirs to the culture of white supremacy that terrorized and lynched African Americans. The culture that made it acceptable for fathers and mothers to bring their own children to witness a barbaric and cruel murder—thereby desensitizing and indoctrinating the next generation and normalizing a culture of violence.

We are the heirs to the trauma of lynching, and the threat of lynching and the impact on families and communities. We must own the fact that fathers and mothers understood they were not safe, and they had to protect their children in any way they could, including teaching them that they were not safe. A lesson that continues to be passed on to this day.

We are the heirs to the silence of the bystanders, some who were horrified and did nothing, and others who understood on some level that to be silent is to condone and protect the status quo.

And we are the heirs to the *courage* of the upstanders. Upstanders who had enough hope to fight. Upstanders such as the members of the NAACP who founded the Memphis chapter in response to Ell Persons's lynching. Upstanders such as Ida B. Wells who spoke, and wrote, and fought against lynching for decades to shine the light of truth. And we are the descendants of the upstanders who remained anonymous, but who courageously resisted in whatever ways they could, to fight for justice. Without their courage and hope, we would not be here today.

By taking responsibility to remember Ell Persons and ensure his story is known, the Students Uniting Memphis of Overton High School's Facing History class are upstanders.

Because we are all here today, we can ask, What does justice for Ell Persons look like? We dedicate this marker today to remember Ell Persons, as a human being, not just a victim, but a son, a brother, a husband, a friend, and a member of our community. Markers, memorials, and statues are a symbol of what story we choose to tell about the past and ourselves. They reflect our values and who we are.

By our willingness to face history and ourselves, we are creating a new narrative. We are saying that we are people willing to take action to heal from the past and to stop modern forms of racial injustice. This won't be easy, but we can do so with hope because we have taken this step today.

History is us.

Building a Toolbox

Essential Questions

- What tools and resources can be used to strengthen our communities and society?
- What tools do I need to use and develop in order to make a difference?

Materials

HANDOUT
Building a Toolbox

Overview

Many Facing History educators, as well as scholars and activists, refer to the "tools" that individuals, groups, and institutions use to create change. These tools might be political, economic, social, or psychological in nature, and we often study how people have used them to create positive and negative change. Part of learning to be civically active is thinking through how change happens. This lesson helps students create a plan for how they might create change, based on what they have studied about changemakers in history and today. While this lesson is not about taking action per se, it is about the important reflection that happens before action, where students recognize or create what they might need in order to make a difference. This exercise in itself can empower students to decide to take action in response to an injustice they witness or an issue they care about.

In this activity, students will consider the "tools" they need in order to effectively participate in creating the kind of community and world they seek (e.g., "eyeglasses to help me focus more clearly"). Through their toolbox, students will create physical representations of the skills, attitudes, and actions that are necessary to strengthen their communities and foster civic engagement. The toolbox will serve as a reminder to them of the importance of their choices and their responsibility to ally with others to contribute to a world that is more caring, just, and equitable.

Notes to Teacher

1. **Different tools are needed to address different goals.** You might align the toolbox with a specific purpose, depending on the content or themes your students are studying. For example:
   - Toolbox for Change
   - Toolbox for Justice
   - Toolbox for Democracy
   - Toolbox for Citizenship
   - Toolbox for Participation
   - Toolbox for Social Responsibility
   - Toolbox for Upstanders

Depending on your unit of study, you might focus on only one, such as "Toolbox for Justice," or you might allow your students to decide on the toolbox that is most needed for a given situation or most important to them.

2. **There are many ways to incorporate toolboxes in the classroom, depending on your goals and time available.** Students can "build" virtual toolboxes as a brainstorming activity, providing a stepping stone to an essay or a class discussion. Or students can actually construct three-dimensional toolboxes that can be shared through a Gallery Walk or presented at a student exhibition (see also the inclusion of a toolbox in a larger culminating project for Gateway Middle School, page 87, or the *Memphis Exploratory: Grade 8 Course Outline*, available at facinghistory.org/ctp-links, which includes as a final project a Toolbox for Strengthening Community.

   Toolbox projects can be based on content covered in class and/or additional research. You might also use the toolbox project after completing the "Leveraging Civic Power" lesson (page 60) and/or reading a selection of CTP readings (beginning on page 28). When students are asked to explain, using evidence, how particular tools can help achieve specific goals, toolbox projects provide an effective way to evaluate student learning at the end of a Facing History unit or course.

3. **While these instructions are designed to introduce the toolbox project, students will likely need additional time either in or out of class to finish the project.** We encourage teachers to set further guidelines and deadlines for this project that meet the needs of their students. Consider designating a space in your classroom or school to display students' completed toolboxes.

Activities

1. Introduce the Toolbox Metaphor

Tell students they will be working on a project that will support them as they choose how they wish to participate in improving and strengthening their community. Begin by brainstorming the purpose of a toolbox and the items that are typically found inside. After students consider how toolboxes are used to build and fix physical structures, ask them to imagine a figurative toolbox that includes tools that can be used to build and fix our communities—school, local, national, and global.

2. Define the Focus of the Toolbox

Pass out (or adapt) the "Building a Toolbox" project handout. At this point, you can either define the type of toolbox students will be constructing (e.g., Toolbox for Upstanders or Toolbox for Participation), or you can provide options for students to choose from. Read the instructions for the project as a whole group and answer any clarifying questions. Then give students the rest of the class to work individually or in small groups on their projects. Consider providing additional class time or assigning the project for homework so students have time to complete it as thoughtfully as possible.

3. Identify Tools

You may want to start out with a reflection as students consider the tools needed to enact change. For example, you might ask students to write a reflection in their journals in response to these questions:

- What "tools"—values, habits of mind, knowledge—do you feel you need in order to participate in the communities around you or address the issues that concern you?

- In what ways do you feel prepared to participate in the communities around you? In what ways do you feel unprepared to participate?

Depending on your students' experience with project-based learning, you may need to create additional scaffolding to help them brainstorm their list of tools, think about how to represent them in their toolboxes, and manage their time. It is always helpful when the teacher provides a model for part of the project to help students visualize abstract concepts. For example, you might create an artifact that represents one of the tools in your toolbox and do a "think aloud" to help students understand your process in coming up with it.

4. Share Toolboxes

Students can learn a great deal from seeing each other's toolboxes. You might have students pair up to discuss their choices with a partner. Or students could showcase their toolboxes to the whole class or school community, as a Gallery Walk, student exhibition, or oral presentations. If time is limited, you may ask each student to share one tool from his or her toolbox with the class. Have students take notes as their classmates share in order to help them remember the variety of tools the class has created.

5. Final Reflection and Debrief

After viewing each other's toolboxes and/or listening to student presentations, provide time for students to reflect in their journals and then hold a class discussion. Sample reflection and/or discussion questions include the following:

- What tools are the most popular? Why might that be the case?

- Which tools seem most accessible? To whom? Who might not have access to these tools? Why?

- Which tools seem out of your reach at the moment, and what could be done to gain access to them?

- Were there any "tools" that you would like to add to your toolbox? If so, what were they and why do you need to add them to your toolbox?

Building a Toolbox

In this project, you will create a real, tangible toolbox that can take a variety of forms: an actual box with a new design or decoration, a hollowed-out old book, a soft-sided sewn object, a picture frame, a shadow box, or something else that represents or relates to your topic. Your "tools" can also take many forms: paintings, collages or other forms of visual art, poems or favorite quotations, or symbolic objects, to name just a few. There are a number of questions that you need to consider when deciding which items to include in your toolbox:

- What will I have in my toolbox that will help me do "small acts" of goodness on a daily basis?

- What will I have in my toolbox that will help me turn those small acts into something bigger and more impactful?

- What will I include in my toolbox that will help me choose kindness over indifference, especially during difficult times?

- What will I need in my toolbox to sustain me when this work gets hard?

- What will I have in my toolbox that will help me remember why this work is necessary?

- What will I have in my toolbox that can help me build connections with people who are different from me?

- What will I have in my toolbox that will help me seek allies and partners to enhance the impact of our efforts?

In addition to the toolbox, you will also complete a short writing assignment that **explains your tools, how you imagine you will use each of them, and how they connect to the world you hope to create** (e.g., the importance of preserving human dignity, choosing kindness over cruelty, fighting against injustice, and breaking ambitious efforts for social change into smaller daily habits).

Your toolbox should:

1. Be a tangible, constructed, creative, three-dimensional box that is filled with at least five items that are your tools.

2. Demonstrate effort, thoughtfulness, and insight into our course of study.

3. Clearly and thoughtfully convey answers to some of the questions listed above, through the tools and possibly the toolbox itself.

4. Be accompanied by a well-composed, thoughtful piece of writing that clearly explains the tools found in your toolbox, their meaning to you, and how they will help you participate in your community to build a just and equitable society.

Leveraging Civic Power

Essential Question

- How can we determine the most effective way to make a difference in our neighborhoods, our nation, and the world? Which strategies are best for bringing about the changes we want to see?

Materials

📖 **READING**
Becoming Literate in Power

📄 **HANDOUT**
Analyzing Levers of Power

📖 **READINGS**
See the CTP readings beginning on page 28

Learning Objectives

- Students will understand that "choosing to participate" often starts with small steps and that simple actions can lead one to become more committed and involved in the future.

- Students will be able to identify some specific ways they might participate in bringing about a positive change in a community to which they belong.

Overview

Most people would agree that engaged citizens are essential to a healthy democracy. But what does it mean to be a good citizen, and how do citizens learn to use their power to make change? Eric Liu, civic entrepreneur, author, and founder of Citizen University, argues that literacy in power is essential to making democracy work. He writes, "The re-imagining of civics as the teaching and learning of *power* is so necessary . . . If you don't learn how to practice power, someone else will do it for you—in your name, on your turf, with your voice, and often against your interests."[6]

Legal scholar Martha Minow has observed that one of the biggest barriers that individuals face in getting involved is that it is hard to know what actual steps to take: "Often times we see something that's unjust and we wonder, 'Where do I go? What do I do?'"[7] In an effort to help individuals identify concrete actions to take when they choose to participate, Minow developed a "levers of power" framework to map out the organizations, institutions, and technologies that can enable us to strengthen the impact of our voices and our actions. In this lesson, students will learn about these "levers" of power and analyze how some individuals and communities have strategically used them to make change. Students will then have the opportunity to think about which levers are most accessible to them personally and how they might use these to bring about changes they would like to see in their own communities.

---

6 Eric Liu, *You're More Powerful than You Think: A Citizen's Guide to Making Change Happen* (*PublicAffairs*, 2017).
7 Facing History and Ourselves, "Martha Minow: Levers of Power" (video), accessed August 26, 2016.

Notes to Teacher

1. You may want to introduce the "levers of power" framework at the start of your course and have students apply a levers of power analysis to specific incidents and actions throughout their study. The levers of power framework can help students collect examples of civic and historic agency and expand their understanding of how different individuals have found and used power to achieve their goals.

Activities

1. **Activate Prior Knowledge**

   Tell students that you are going to be talking about citizen power in democracies. Ask them what words and images come to mind when they hear the phrase *citizen power*. What might be some examples of citizen power from the history they have studied or current events? What does citizen power look like and sound like? (Students may mention political campaigns, voting, protests, petitions, and other examples.)

2. **Read "Becoming Literate in Power"**

   In this reading, Eric Liu discusses how students can become "literate" in civic power. (Depending on students' reading level, you may want to use the Chunking or Annotating and Paraphrasing strategy.) Use the Save the Last Word for Me teaching strategy (see facinghistory.org/ctp-links) to have students examine and discuss the reading. After all students have had an opportunity to respond, you could reconvene as a class and ask students: How does Liu define *power*? What does it mean to be "literate" in power? How is literacy in power similar to literacy in reading and writing? Who do you think has power in your community? How did they get it?

3. **Introduce "Levers of Power"**

   - Explain to students that they are going to think about what it takes to get involved in making their school, community, and country better, more equitable places. Explain that one of the biggest barriers that individuals face in getting involved is that it is hard to know what actual steps to take. As legal scholar Martha Minow puts it: "Oftentimes we see something that's unjust and we wonder, 'Where do I go? What do I do?'"

   - Now explain to students that they will look at a framework for planning what to do in order to respond to injustice and make positive changes in society.

   - Distribute the handout "Analyzing Levers of Power." Spend a moment exploring the metaphor of the lever in the title. Ask students to define the meaning of the word *lever*, and then ask them to make an inference about what the phrase "levers of power" might mean. Tell students that in a literal sense, a lever is a tool that allows one to pick up or move something much heavier than could be lifted without it. In other words, a lever allows someone to use a small amount of force to have a big impact.

- Briefly walk students through each category on the second side of the handout, which outlines the individuals, organizations, and technology platforms that can have this sort of amplifying effect at a societal level. By influencing or making use of these "levers," individuals might have a larger impact on their community or society.

- Ask students to come up with examples of individuals or groups that belong to each category in order to make sure that everyone understands them. Do all people have equal access to all the levers? What influences who can and can't access them?

4. **Analyze Strategies for Making Change**

   Students will use the "levers of power" framework to analyze examples of individuals who "chose to participate." For this activity, you will need some examples for students to analyze. You can select from the readings starting on page 28, or you can apply the framework to upstanders in the content you have been studying.

   - In teams of two, assign students one of the CTP readings or ask them to choose from a selection that you have curated.

   - After they are assigned or choose their reading, pairs should read and answer the questions on the first side of the handout "Analyzing Levers of Power."

   - In each row on the second side of the handout, students should write a sentence or two explaining how the individual(s) in the reading used the lever described in the heading. If such a lever was not used, students can write "N/A" in the row. If a lever of power was involved that is not listed on the handout, students should describe it at the bottom of the page.

5. **Share "Levers of Power" Analyses**

   - After students have completed their handouts, have them meet briefly with a classmate who worked with a different reading. When they meet, they should introduce the story they each read, describe the strategies that the people they read about used, and explain which levers of power were most useful to those people. Time permitting, ask students to change partners one or two more times so that they can learn about additional examples of choosing to participate.

   - Finally, lead a whole-group discussion in which you ask students to share their observations. Guide the discussion with the following questions:

     - What patterns did you notice? Did certain "levers of power" seem to come up in more readings than others?

     - Which of the strategies for change that you learned about seem most effective? Most difficult? Most creative?

     - Which of the levers of power on the handout seem most accessible to you? Which seem most difficult to influence? Which are you struggling to understand?

6. Apply the Levers of Power to Civic Action Projects

- You can use the "levers of power" framework to help students strategize about a larger civic action project (see Sample CTP Projects and Assignments beginning on page 79). Once students have chosen an issue that they care about and a change they would like to bring about regarding that issue, ask them to describe some specific actions they could take to try to help make that change happen. Their plans should include at least two of the "levers" of power outlined in this lesson, and students should describe how the specific action they could take might make use of those levers to increase their impact.

Becoming Literate in Power

The following excerpt is from an interview by Facing History with civic entrepreneur Eric Liu, founder of Citizen University and author of *You're More Powerful Than You Think: A Citizen's Guide to Making Change Happen* (PublicAffairs, 2017).

I think one of the most important things we have to do right now, everyday Americans, is to become literate in power. I mean that not just as a metaphor. I mean that almost literally: You have to know how to *read* power and you have to know how to *write* power.

To read power means understanding, in any situation, why your neighborhood is the way it is, why certain people get certain resources, why certain schools get funding and others don't, why the bus line goes to this block and not that block, why nobody seems to clean up this park but two streets over they get everything they want. Understanding and reading the map of power means understanding who has money power, who has people power, who has the power of ideas, who has the power of influence to change social norms, and to be able to read that map truly is a matter of literacy. Understanding part of that is understanding decision-makers in government, but part of it also is about influentials, whether they are faith leaders or elders or businesspeople or other folks. People who have respect in the community. Being able to read that map is an important part of power literacy.

How do you write power? Once you can read the map of who *has* power and through what conduits in a community different forms of power flow, then you've got to make a determination that "I want to be part of that picture. I want to write myself into the map. I want to rewrite that map." Which means that you yourself have to become committed to get involved and participate: to show up in government, to show up in the life of your block or your neighborhood organizations. Simply by the act of organizing and participating you learn how to write power.

That doesn't mean that overnight you're going to be able to change society. That doesn't mean that if you get involved in certain campaigns to change something or grassroots efforts to build something in a neighborhood that you're going to succeed all the time. But it does mean that simply by practicing, you get better, and simply by participating, you learn how to write power as well as how to read it.

. . . As the title of my book says, *You're More Powerful Than You Think*. This is not just a subject matter for insiders or people who already have clout and people who are well known, this is a message that you, as a young person in a community that might be off the mainstream media's grid, you have the power to change attitudes, to change conditions, and to change politics where you live and in ways that radiate out from where you live. . . .

Analyzing Levers of Power

Reading name:

1. What change did the individual(s) in this reading want to make?

2. What strategies did the individual(s) use in order to make the change happen?

3. Which powerful people or organizations ("levers of power") did the individual(s) attempt to influence?

4. Which strategies led to the most success? Which failed?

Describe a strategy you observed in your reading that addresses each lever of power listed below. If the subject of your reading does not attempt to use one of the levers, write "N/A" next to it.

Lever of Power	Strategy
Government (National, State, Local)	
Nonprofit Organizations/ Charities	
Industry/Commercial Organizations	
Professional Media	
Social Media/Internet	
Schools and Education	
Influential Individuals (Authors, Lecturers, etc.)	

FACING HISTORY AND OURSELVES   www.facinghistory.org

10 Questions for Young Changemakers

Note: The following lessons are excerpted from the unit 10 Questions for Young Changemakers, developed in collaboration with the Democratic Knowledge Project at Harvard University. The full unit, available at facinghistory.org/ctp-links, includes three cases of student activism:

- The 1963 Chicago Public Schools boycott
- The 1968 East Los Angeles student walkout
- The movement against gun violence launched by Parkland high school students in 2018

Essential Question

- What is the 10 Questions for Young Changemakers framework?

Materials

📄 **HANDOUT**
Are You a Changemaker?

Teaching Strategies

(see facinghistory.org/ctp-links)
Using Journals in a CTP Project
Think, Pair, Share

Overview

How can young people change the world? How can we use digital media effectively and safely when we "choose to participate"? By exploring these essential questions, students make important connections between the historical and contemporary case studies they examine and their own civic participation. We do not expect students to determine a single, "correct" answer. Essential questions are rich and open-ended; they are designed to be revisited over time, and as students explore the content in greater depth, they may find themselves emerging with new ideas, understanding, and questions.

Part 1: Getting to Know the 10 Questions

Learning Objectives

- Students will identify the main ideas of the 10 Questions Framework.
- Students will connect the 10 Questions Framework to their experience.

Overview

Conventional approaches to teaching civics and democratic participation often begin with topics such as the branches of government or the lawmaking process. This approach is distant from the lives and experiences of young people, and it can fail to engage students. That's why the 10 Questions Framework begins with a student-centered question: "What do you care about, and why does it matter to you?" This is designed to spark students' interest and help them think about civic engagement in terms of their own identities and passions. This lesson asks students to respond to that question, and then it introduces them to the framework as a whole.

Context

What Can the 10 Questions Tell Us about Civic Agency in a Digital Age?

Ordinary people can participate in the political process and drive social change in ways well beyond voting—they can raise funds, mobilize others to get involved, protest, deliberate, and work on public issues. Digital technology has had a dramatic impact on these traditional forms of political engagement, and young people stand to benefit greatly from these changes in civic action and the social changes such innovation might inspire. But the digital environment comes with risks: privacy breaches, anonymous trolls, polarization, "fake news," and cyberbullying are all too common in the digital public sphere. How can educators help young people develop into equitable, effective, and self-protective civic actors in a digital age?

The 10 Questions Framework provides an effective approach to meeting these recent changes in political engagement. The framework is designed to engage young people with the ethical concerns of citizenship, focusing on equity, effectiveness, and self-protection to ease the burdens of participation.

Equitable participation. Young people engage in important civic work online and off, no matter who they are. But citizenship also entails identifying, curating, and elevating the voices of those who lack the opportunity to participate. The 10 Questions Framework looks to connect students with the norms of accuracy, authenticity, equity, and openness to diversity essential to democratic action. You can't have quality participation without equality.

Effective participation. Participation is effective when individual participants can point to something that has changed on account of their efforts—a representative's vote, a new policy, media attention to an issue, or even a friend's shifted perspective. In this way, individual activities can help to shape the attitudes of entire communities. The 10 Questions Framework engages students by asking how their actions can be effective and what counts as effective in the first place.

Self-protective participation. Security online goes beyond privacy settings. The publicity and permanence of digital communication requires civic actors to think about the digital afterlife of their choices. How can young people preserve their psychological well-being in the face of unpredictable consequences of digital participation, the dangers that come with public exposure, and collisions between their speech online and their lives offline? By helping students analyze the risks and rewards of political participation, the

10 Questions Framework offers them opportunities to learn how to be safe and sustainable political actors in their own lives.

Notes to Teacher

1. **Preparing to Teach the 10 Questions Framework**

   Before beginning the first lesson, it is strongly recommended that teachers familiarize themselves with the 10 Questions for Young Changemakers framework. The 10 Questions website (at yppactionframe.fas.harvard.edu) introduces relevant examples of the structured implementation of the framework, moving from understanding to inquiry to action. It is important for teachers to understand how the 10 Questions Framework supports young people in the development of equitable, effective, and self-protective civic agency.

Activities

1. **Begin with Question 1: "Why Does It Matter to Me?"**

   - Ask students to take five minutes to write in their journals about an issue in the world that matters to them. Ask:
     - Why is the issue important to you personally?
     - Why would you like to see change on this particular issue?
   - Once students have finished journaling, ask them to share their thoughts with a partner in a Think, Pair, Share format.

2. **Transition into a Whole-Class Discussion**

   - Ask some volunteers to share their issue. As students share, ask the class to brainstorm some ways they might involve themselves (big or small) in the process of bringing about change on that issue. Record students' ideas on the board.

3. **Introduce Students to the 10 Questions Framework**

   - Tell your students that this series of questions is designed to help people effectively and safely "choose to participate." Share the "Are You a Changemaker?" handout with students, which includes the following questions:
     - Why does it matter to me?
     - How much should I share?
     - How do I make it about more than myself?
     - Where do we start?
     - How can we make it easy and engaging for others to join in?
     - How do we get wisdom from crowds?
     - How do we handle the downside of crowds?
     - Are we pursuing voice or influence or both?

- How do we get from voice to change?

- How can we find allies?

- Next, explain to students that at the beginning of the class, they already began to answer Questions 1 (Why does it matter to me?) and 4 (Where do we start?) about an issue that is important to them. Let students pick one additional question (other than 1 or 4) from the framework to reflect on further. Then ask them to spend five minutes journaling in response to the following prompts:

  - Paraphrase the question in your own words.

  - Why might the question help young people who are planning to take action on an issue of importance to them?

  - What questions do you have about it?

- Ask students to pair up and share their responses in a Think, Pair, Share format.

Are You a Changemaker?

Do you want to develop equitable, effective, self-protective civic-political agency?[1]

10 Questions for Participatory Politics

1. Why does it matter to me?

What do you care about? What is your passion? Where does it come from? Start with the experiences and interests you and your friends already can't get enough of, and connect that engagement to civic and political themes.

2. How much should I share?

What kind of risk should you take for the things you care about? Consider how much you should share. Which part of your persona do you want to be shared publicly? Help your community consider how different audiences may react to their posts and how a post might impact them years down the road.

3. How do I make it about more than myself?

How can you and your community take it from "I" to "we"? Help your users think of themselves as part of something bigger. Can you expand the network of engagement for yourself and your users by actively rewarding authenticity, accuracy, truth-telling, and bridge-building across social divides?

4. Where do we start?

Go where your peers go. Can you make use of spaces where you and your friends and associates already gather to connect and pursue shared interests?

5. How can we make it easy and engaging for others to join in?

Remember that some engagement is better than none. Where are the opportunities for light-touch engagement that is potentially powerful in itself and also a possible gateway into deeper involvement?

6. How do we get wisdom from crowds?

Invite investigation and critique. Create openings for your friends, associates, and even strangers to dig into, verify, challenge, and contribute to the knowledge base you provide and stay open to evolving purposes.

7. How do we handle the downside of crowds?

Be prepared for people to say and do things you don't like in your shared space. The goal is to keep your community open and democratic, and that also means protecting it from those who would misuse that freedom and opportunity.

---

1   Harvard University's Democratic Knowledge Project created this explanation of the 10 Questions Framework.

8. Are we pursuing voice or influence or both?

Raising awareness is key. It is already an important civic and political action. Are you also trying to drive change beyond that point? You'll need that awareness to elevate civic and political engagement over time.

9. How do we get from voice to change?

Is your goal to convert voice to influence over policies, institutions, or concrete practices? If so, you'll need to move beyond raising awareness to mobilize specific actions on the basis of the attention you manage to get.

10. How can we find allies?

How can you engage with power holders in a way that benefits your cause and also empowers you? Get connected with allies who can provide mentorship and broker on your behalf, being creative in your methods and seeking elites in a variety of places—sometimes beyond the usual suspects.

FACING HISTORY AND OURSELVES   www.facinghistory.org

Part 2: Applying the Questions to Civic Action Projects

Essential Question

- How can the 10 Questions Framework help you plan a course of action to address an issue or problem that you care about?

Materials

📄 **HANDOUT**
Quotations from Changemakers

📄 **HANDOUT**
10 Questions Framework:
Questions for Me

Teaching Strategies

(see facinghistor y.org/ctp-links)
Concentric Circles

Learning Objectives

- Students will define an issue that matters to them and identify short- and long-term goals for enacting change on that issue.

- Students will spell out the specific strategies to achieve their goals that align with their long-term and short-term visions.

Overview

While this lesson provides a framework for introducing final projects, it does not offer explicit guidance on how to design a project. For this reason, before implementing this lesson, teachers need to be clear about what types of action-oriented projects they want to pursue with their students. They will also need to consider how they will tailor the 10 Questions Framework to the interests and needs of their students.

Notes to Teacher

1. **Implementing Civic Action Projects**

   The purpose of this lesson is to circle back to students' interests and passions on a specific issue and have them conceive of ways to enact change on that issue using the 10 Questions Framework. Teachers will likely need to devote additional class periods to introduce the project and provide time for student collaboration to complete it. For suggestions, see Sample CTP Projects and Assignments beginning on page 79. You may also want to refer to the "levers of power" framework, included in the Leveraging Civic Power lesson on page 60.

2. Post-Project Reflection

We encourage teachers to structure sufficient time for students to debrief their projects and provide feedback to each other. The following prompts might be helpful to consider when planning a debrief process for your students:

- What was the issue your project aimed to tackle?
- What were the short-term and long-term goals of your project?
- What strategies did you use?
- How did your project incorporate the 10 Questions Framework?
- Overall, how did your project go? What challenges did you face, and how did you respond to them?
- If you could do the project over again, what changes would you make?
- What counts as success for your project?

Activities

1. Define an Issue

Open the lesson by asking students to reflect on what it means to take civic action. Pass out the handout "Quotations from Changemakers" and ask students to respond to one or more of these quotes in their journals. Students can respond to the quote in any way they choose, including explaining why it resonates with them, what they like or dislike about it, or its intended meaning.

Once students have responded privately, ask them to return to their initial responses to Questions 1 and 2 from the framework, which they began to explore in Part 1: "What do I care about?" and "Why does it matter to me?" Tell students to reread their previous answers and underline one to three sentences that they want to dig into more deeply. Next, have students start a new entry that explores one of the sentences they underlined. They might write about new understanding, raise new questions, or expand on personal connections to the material. Time allowing, invite volunteers to share ideas from their reflections with the class.

2. Connect to the 10 Questions Framework

- Pass out copies of the "10 Questions Framework: Questions for Me" handout. Tell students that they will explore their ideas from Part 1 in more detail in a new response on their handouts (Questions 1 and 2).

- Once students have identified an issue that matters to them, ask them to detail the goals that they want to achieve on that issue. Ask them to identify both a short-term and long-term goal (Question 3 on the handout).

- Ask students to select two or three questions from the 10 Questions Framework that will most help them achieve their short- and long-term goals (Question 4 on the handout). For instance, if a student's goal is to accomplish policy change on a specific issue, they may want to choose Framework Question 9 "How do we get from voice to change? and Framework Question 10 ("How do we find allies?").

- Once students have chosen their questions, give them time to think about how they will address the questions through specific actions. For instance, if they want to address Framework Question 10, they may want to co-sponsor a forum with local community organizations. Students should write their ideas in the column marked "Answer."

- Debrief students' responses to the questions on the handout using the Concentric Circles strategy so that students have the opportunity to share ideas with a number of different classmates. Then give them time to add any new ideas to their handouts.

- To close the lesson, ask students to reflect on the following quote from civil rights activist Franklin McCain: "Inevitably, people will ask me, 'What can I do?' What kind of question is that? Look around you. Once you identify what you want to do, don't ask for the masses to help you because they won't come."

    - How do you interpret McCain's quote?

    - What have you learned from this unit that will help you heed McCain's advice?

Quotations from Changemakers

Directions: Respond to one or more of the following quotes in your journal or in the space below.

"If you have come here to help me, you are wasting your time. But if you have come because your liberation is bound up with mine, then let us work together."

—Aboriginal activists group, Queensland, Australia, 1970s

"What you're supposed to do when you don't like a thing is change it. If you can't change it, change the way you think about it. Don't complain."

—Maya Angelou, poet

"Injustice anywhere is a threat to justice everywhere. We are caught in an inescapable network of mutuality, tied in a single garment of destiny. Whatever affects one directly, affects all indirectly."

—Martin Luther King Jr., minister and civil rights activist

"Sometimes change comes not in the first round, but at the second, third or fourth. Change starts with one person questioning, challenging, speaking up and doing something to make a difference. We can each make a difference . . . because each of us is already part of the community where racism exists and thrives."

—Paul Kivel, writer, educator, activist

10 Questions Framework: Questions for Me

Directions: Record your answers in the spaces below.

Question	Answer
1. What do I care about?	
2. Why does it matter to me?	
3. What is a short-term goal I hope to achieve on my issue(s)? A long-term goal? How might I spread awareness? What small actions could I take to achieve these goals?	
4. My two to three questions from the 10 Questions Framework: How will I address these questions with specific actions?	

Sample CTP Projects and Assignments

CTP Project Spotlights

You may choose to wrap up your history, literature, or humanities unit with culminating reflection activities and a structured assignment, such as completing "**levers of power**" analyses on a selection of **CTP readings** or using the **Public Memory and the Role of Memorials** or **Building a Toolbox** lesson. Teachers sometimes approach the end of a Facing History unit with flexibility and creativity, as students may be inspired to invest themselves in a class project, or series of projects, to make a difference in their school, community, country, or the world.

We urge you to follow students' passion and energy, to be willing to deviate from your planned activities, and to use the resources included in these pages to help guide projects in the school, community, and beyond that are conceived, created, and led by your students. If such energy does not emerge from the class, you cannot force it, and it does not mean that you have failed to produce the desired outcome. Every class is different, and the effects of the learning and growth students experienced in your unit may not reveal themselves until some time has passed, perhaps even when the students are adults.

The spotlights included on these pages illustrate just a few examples of how CTP has come to life in the classroom or in the lives of students. We look forward to hearing yours.

Developing Civic Agency and Purpose through Studying History

Iyonna M., a 9th-grader at Lincoln Park High School in Chicago, reflected on the lessons she learned in middle school, when her class explored both the historical context and the personal choices of individuals in Facing History's case-study units *Holocaust and Human Behavior, Choices in Little Rock,* and *Democracy in Action: A Study Guide to the film "Freedom Riders."*

"When I think about how risky and scary it must have been for the Freedom Riders to stand up for their own rights, I think, How can I *not* do something, much less risky, and stand up when *I* see injustice?

"The people that we read about were real, and the choices that they made were important. Through their personal stories it became clear to me that my own actions matter. . . . The courage and persistence of the Freedom Riders was extraordinary. . . . I use this as an example to feed my hunger, to learn more about my community and find opportunities to serve it. I want to help people understand that when they hurt, they can turn it into a strength to drive them to want to do better for themselves. The same way the Freedom Riders did in the past. The work that took place [in my middle school class] helps me respond to injustice. . . . I hope to carry these lessons with me all my life."

Righting an Injustice

At Santa Monica High School, a group of students in a freshman seminar took a look at their school community and uncovered a hidden-in-plain-sight injustice they wanted to challenge.

They had just learned about the troubling history of eugenics in the United States through Facing History's *Race and Membership in American History* and other resources, including *No Más Bebés*, a documentary about the forced sterilization of Latina women in Los Angeles County and USC Medical Center in the 1960s and 1970s. When students were then challenged to connect their studies to current needs in the community, a group of 9th-grade girls noticed that some low-income students were not coming to school when they had their periods. Could it be because they didn't have supplies to bring to school, where they were charged 25 cents?

When students researched the problem and possible solutions, they found that—on paper—it didn't seem like there was a large population in need. However, they also observed that many students felt the stigma of signing up for the free and reduced lunch program, which impacts funding that could provide access to hygienic products.

The students then identified a company, Aunt Flow, from which they could purchase dispensers to place in bathrooms across campus to provide free supplies. They negotiated a discounted price for the dispensers and materials and figured out the total cost to supply all the bathrooms on campus. With the facts in hand, they presented their proposal to the Board of Education. Their argument: "If I get a bloody finger at school, I can get a band-aid, so what is the difference if I'm a girl and I get my period?" The Board gave the students close to $7,000 to purchase the dispensers. Not content to simply celebrate their success, the students then formed a club to act as a watchdog over the project, ensuring that the Board followed up on its commitments.

If You Name It, You Can Be It

Do words have the power to influence the choices people make? Two students, Sarah D. and Monica M., from Watchung Hills Regional High School in New Jersey think they can. In 2014 in their Facing History class, they were reading stories of "upstanders," a term coined by diplomat Samantha Power and used by Facing History to identify people who have chosen to make a difference in the world by speaking out against injustice and creating positive change. But when Sarah and Monica were working on a speech for school, their computer repeatedly flagged *upstander* as a misspelling. As they looked in different dictionaries, they realized that "this groundbreaking term, one that has inspired our own local community to eschew intolerance, is technically not an official English word."[1]

In that moment they decided to launch a campaign to get *upstander*, a word that "is critical to the well-being of our society,"[2] added to the dictionary. To accomplish this, they created a Change.org petition to gather support and bring awareness of their cause to the *Oxford* and *Merriam-Webster* dictionaries. Their petition gathered hundreds of signatures online, and their campaign caught the attention of several New Jersey lawmakers.

1 Sarah Decker and Monica Mahal, "Define Upstander," *Not in Our Town* blog, entry posted October 22, 2014, accessed October 16, 2015.
2 Ibid.

In June 2015, the New Jersey legislature approved a resolution that declared the state's support for the campaign to include *upstander* in both of the dictionaries. Soon the dictionary publishers responded: "Oxford University Press frequently receives requests from members of the public to add a particular word to our dictionaries, but an official legislative resolution supporting a word's inclusion may be unprecedented."[3]

The Oxford University Press added *upstander* to its list of words for potential inclusion in February 2016 and began to monitor how frequently the word was used in publications and public speeches. In December 2016, *upstander* was added to the *Oxford English Dictionary* as a direct result of the campaign begun by Sarah and Monica.

Responding to Current Events

When students develop a sense of civic agency, they are better prepared to respond to events as they happen, within or outside of the classroom. In August 2017, a student from Malden, Massachusetts, shattered a glass panel of the New England Holocaust Memorial in Boston. The fact that the student was from Malden troubled his peers at Malden High School, where students experience Facing History's *Holocaust and Human Behavior* case study. They decided to act.

A group of Malden High students worked with the school's lead history teacher, principal, and superintendent, as well as the city mayor, to set up a special event at the Holocaust Memorial that September, preceding the opening of an art exhibit of *Stolpersteine*, or "stumbling stones," which memorialize those who experienced Nazi persecution, that was opening nearby at Boston City Hall. At the event, to which they invited Holocaust survivors, community members, and other officials, students read short statements about why they believed it was important to remember the Holocaust, and some spoke about their own family connections to Holocaust survivors.

Then, after three local Holocaust survivors spoke, together they walked through the Holocaust Memorial with the survivors and then went to Boston City Hall for the opening of the *Stolpersteine* exhibit. The students also launched a fundraising initiative to purchase stumbling stones in memory of Malden residents. As one senior said after the event, "We wanted to make something positive out of it. This [vandalism] does not represent all of us. It only represents one person's actions. We wanted to make up for that."[4]

Choosing to Vote

For over 20 years, the Memphis office of Facing History and Ourselves has run a Student Leadership Group (SLG) program. What started with one high school now includes students from over 15 high schools from across the city who, each year, are trained in topics that include how to facilitate difficult conversations, confront bullying and ostracism, learn from upstanders in history, and become civically informed leaders today.

---

3 Oxford Dictionaries, "Legislation meets lexicography: The campaign for dictionary recognition of the word 'upstander,'" *OxfordWords* (blog), entry posted July 24, 2015, accessed October 16, 2015.

4 Penny Schwartz, "Malden students, teachers honor Shoah victims at memorial," *Jewish Journal*, September 22, 2017, accessed November 14, 2019.

The 2018 Student Leadership Group decided to focus on a student-led, nonpartisan voting initiative. Although it was agreed that the initiative would be designed to increase voter participation, whether that meant reducing barriers to voting or registering new voters was unclear at the start. Through research, it became clear that many Memphis groups already focus on voter registration, yet registered voters don't always vote. So the overall goal that emerged was to *re-engage* voters: to target people who are eligible and registered to vote but who have not been voting.

The group explored case studies of youth activism and the historic struggle for voting rights, using the 10 Questions for Young Changemakers framework. And then they applied what they had learned to the question of how students could go about re-engaging voters. They decided that their core strategy would be persuasion, and their tactics would be personal relationships, education, and FOMO (fear of missing out). The name of the campaign would be Engage Memphis, with social media handles #Engage901Vote (901 is the local area code) and @engagememphis.

The SLG then spread their campaign idea to other schools, again using the 10 Questions Framework to help shape and sharpen students' action plans. To help students track and quantify their efforts, and to concretely garner commitment from the people they were persuading, they created a voter pledge that the students tracked online, tying back to the key question from the 10 Questions Framework: "How do we make it easy and engaging for others to get involved?"

People completed the pledge in three ways—a paper handout, an online form, or through a QR code—and they were encouraged to share that they took the pledge on social media.

CHOOSE TO VOTE
I choose to vote.
I choose to vote for the youth.
I choose to vote for my community.
I choose to vote for a future where all can thrive.
I choose to vote for my parents, neighbors, and future generations.
I choose to use my voice to empower those who cannot speak for themselves.
I choose to vote because my vote is my voice.

As a result of their involvement in this project, many students began to think differently about the importance of voting:

"I came in thinking that voting was not as important, and I am leaving with a better understanding of its impact."

"I came in thinking that voting wasn't really important to me. I leave thinking our vote matters."

"I came thinking this would be hard. I leave knowing it's possible."

Hacking the Future

Sometimes instead of focusing on solving a current issue today, civic action can be about jumping over perceived obstacles and imagining a vision for the future that you can drive toward. In San Francisco, students have been doing just that. In 2016, Facing History's San Francisco office began hosting an annual Student Civic Hackathon to answer the question, How can we transform our communities and increase civic participation through digital innovation? Each spring, students from across the San Francisco Bay Area come together with volunteers from the community for a day of "hacking" social justice issues.

Hacking is creative problem solving; it's an energetic and energizing way to surface lots of ideas (and doesn't actually require the application of technology). "Civic hacking" is a term used to describe design thinking and collaborative activities that lead to civic innovation. Civic hackathons provide an opportunity for participants to learn something new and make some headway on community issues they are interested in.

For the Facing History civic hackathons, students work in teams of four to five and choose a Facing History–themed challenge to focus on:

- **Historical Memory/Legacy:** How should we remember and face our own history? How can we use technology to bring the past alive in ways that could inform our world today?

- **Upstanders:** How can we encourage more people to be upstanders and not bystanders?

- **Stereotyping:** How can technology help reduce stereotyping and labeling of others?

- **Empathy:** How can technology be used to increase empathy within our own communities?

Once students have chosen their theme, they work together to develop a prototype connected to their challenge question. Their solution can fall into one of six categories:

- **Service:** Work with users directly to create an impact
- **Hardware Product:** A replicable solution you can physically touch
- **Software Product:** A set of coded instructions (like an app or program)
- **Instructable:** Step-by-step instructions to help others build your solution on Instructables.com
- **Open Source Code:** Code that can be used and altered by anyone
- **Public Art:** Impact people through creative expression

After a couple of hours of brainstorming and innovating, each team develops a pitch (complete with hashtag) and presents its prototype to the judges, answering three key questions:

- How does your innovation address the challenge question?
- What is the impact on the community or a particular audience?
- How will it lead to a more humane and just society?

Some examples of prototypes from past hackathons include

- an ethical "app" to help rethink stereotyping (#DiscoverEthical);
- an app along with a public kiosk where people could upload stories of upstanders (#DoGoodBeWell);
- a public billboard campaign to increase empathy among different socioeconomic communities in the Bay Area (#WeGotEachOther); and
- Holographic History, holograms in public spaces that could educate others on local history (#SeeItToBelieveIt).

To watch students in action during one of these civic hackathons, see the video "Facing History Hacks: Connecting Social Justice, History, and Technology" at facinghistory.org /ctp-links. While this example is bringing together students from across the city, working with community volunteers, the civic hackathon model can be effectively implemented on any scale and in any venue—in a classroom or a school, or at a public library, community partner, or local business.

Educators who have participated in Facing History's hackathons have gone on to bring the activity into their classroom as a way to jump-start students' thinking and creativity. Teacher Alanna Baumert from Lighthouse Community Charter School in Oakland brought 16 students to the first hackathon. Her response? "I'm here thinking: How can I bring this into my classroom every year? To have a very much hands-on, idea-generating project that puts the focus back on them as changemakers." And you can follow this type of creative idea generation with a Someday/Monday reflection routine to help students think about smaller steps they can take today to realize their vision for tomorrow.

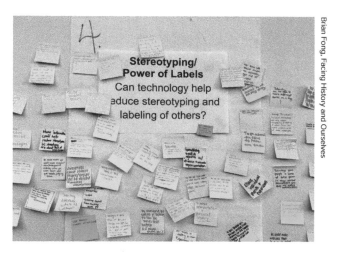

Brian Fong, Facing History and Ourselves

Brian Fong, Facing History and Ourselves

To kick off the civic hackathon, students quickly brainstorm ideas in response to different themes and challenge questions.

After brainstorming, students break into teams to narrow down their ideas and develop their project prototype.

Sample Assignments from Partner Schools

The sample CTP assignments that follow come from members of the Facing History Partner Schools Network. The Partner Schools Network (PSN) is made up of over 140 schools that embrace Facing History's core themes as foundational to the school's mission and weave Facing History content, pedagogy, and teaching strategies throughout the entire school: in classes, advisory groups, faculty meetings, and school community activities.

The PSN is defined by a set of common principles:

- We value the complexities of identity and combat prejudice in our school community.
- We examine choices of the past and their legacies to inform our choices today.
- We integrate intellectual rigor, emotional engagement, and ethical reflection.
- We foster dialogue, empathy, and civic participation.

In addition to integrating Facing History core case studies and units—which include CTP readings and activities—at different grade levels, many schools in the Partner Schools Network create CTP-oriented projects as culminating events of the school year, designed in part to create awareness and foster conversation among peers and the school community. Three of these schools have generously shared their Choosing to Participate project assignments for other educators to use for inspiration and models.

Final Exhibition Project, 8th-Grade Humanities

This month-long final project at Gateway Middle School in San Francisco, California, is the culminating activity of a year-long humanities course focused on the questions: What does it mean to belong? Who decides if you belong? How do people gain belonging? Because the project is the culmination of their study of US history and English language arts, it consists of a written element, a presentation (tri-fold poster and "toolbox"), and research on history and current events. Students present their posters and research at an exhibition night to friends, family, community members, and staff. The school's ultimate goal is to create civically engaged young adults.

In order to develop the understanding and skills to take on such a project at the end of 8th grade, Gateway students use Facing History's resources (including *Choices in Little Rock* and "*Teaching Warriors Don't Cry*") and scope and sequence to:

- Investigate history through the lens of identity, focusing on different novels and eras in US history

- Dig deeper into case studies that help students understand the intersection between laws, social issues, and identity

- Provide students with creative outlets to express and expand upon injustices (e.g., an earlier historical fiction narrative assignment and an activism-through-art project)

- Plan for and respond to issues of intolerance/misconceptions related to identity in their own community

- And, finally, undertake the final exhibition project, an inquiry into fighting for social justice in the United States

The design for this project allows for student choice while providing a highly structured process to give them adequate support to complete the project. Students work in small groups of two to four based on student interest, choosing from a list of possible topics. They are provided with an assignment that outlines deliverables, topic options, a calendar of due dates, and a detailed explanation for each element of their project. After they take a survey stating their top choices of the different project options, students are placed in small groups. Students also have access to a Google Drive folder that contains their project prompt and subsequent worksheets that help to organize student research, create their argument, outline their research paper, and complete their citations. Overall, the project takes place over five weeks, about five hours per week in class.

The project assignment and rubrics (for the exhibition essay, the toolbox and tri-fold, and the students' presentation) are included on the pages that follow.

This sample project is reproduced with permission from Elizabeth Colen and Lucy Hilarides at Gateway Middle School, San Francisco, CA.

Name: _____   Date _____

What social injustices exist in our society and how do we fight them?

Project Description

For your final 8th-grade exhibition project, you will work in small groups to choose a **social justice issue**. This will be an inquiry project tracing the evolution of an issue over the course of history while making claims about how to improve the issue in society today.

You will pick a social issue to research in depth. You will start by identifying the issue and describing why it is a problem. You will then research where the issue came from—when did the problem develop in the history of America? How did it change over the course of time? What laws, people, tactics, or movements created the change?

In order to show the social change, you will pick one data point and consider how things have changed over the nineteenth, twentieth, and twenty-first centuries. Finally, you will report on the current state of the issue in today's society. What still needs to be done? What can we do to continue improving the lives of people affected by this issue?

Topic Choices

- Mass incarceration
- Educational equality
- Gender equality
- LGBTQ equality
- Housing and urban development
- Immigration

- Refugee crisis
- Climate change
- Chicano rights
- Disability rights
- Workers' rights

Project Must-Haves

Your final project will include the following:

1. **Tri-fold Poster:** Project board that includes a visual explanation of your research and findings.

2. **Data Analysis:** What metric will you use to show change? Locate and analyze data that supports your claim. Explain how this data shows social change and why you chose to represent it this way.

3. **Toolbox:** A kit of tangible items to represent how people went about and can continue the social change. Think of it like a toolbox—perhaps a pencil and paper to petition, or a newspaper to represent the media used to raise awareness.

4. **Research Report:** A written component that answers the project question about your social issue (a five-paragraph essay written by each team member).

Deadlines

- Choose your topic   April 8
- Project launch/research begins   April 22 or 23
- Exhibition research notetaker due   May 1
- Draft of essay due   May 14
- Final essay due   May 20
- Final touches to project   May 20
- Mock presentations   May 21 and 22
- Exhibition Night   May 22

Roles and Responsibilities

It will be important to communicate and collaborate on this project, but also to divide and conquer! Elect a "captain" for each element of the project:

_____ Toolbox and Explanations

_____ Research Notes and Outline

_____ Tri-fold Board and Materials

	As a group	Individually
Research	At least 9 sources (if a group of 4, you need 12) Make sure you are not doubling up on sources or information	3 reliable sources, with 5 facts/quotes from each
Essay	Collaborate on the outline Collaborate on your citation page	Write your own essay in your own words
Toolbox	Create items and explanations together	Be able to explain all items in your presentation
Tri-fold	Create an engaging board, share the responsibility of bringing in resources, make sure the presentation is neat and professional	Be able to explain everything on your tri-fold and answer questions about your topic

Displaying and Analyzing Data & Evidence

Goal: To identify and display data and evidence to help support your claim about how your issue has evolved and what still needs to be done.

Key Questions

- How can we identify appropriate data and evidence?
  - Appropriate data comes from a **reliable source**.
  - Appropriate data is evidence that **supports our claim** about how our person/group caused social change.

- What do we do with our data once we have collected it?
  1. **Display** it in a way that is easy to read and analyze (i.e., identify *similarities, differences, trends, and other relationships*, or the lack of, in the data), e.g., through:
     - Tables
     - Charts
     - Bar graphs
     - Line graphs
     - Scatter plots
     - Pie charts
  2. **Analyze** the *similarities, differences, trends, and other relationships*, or the lack of, in the data. Does the data support your claim? If so, how and why?

Displaying Data Checklist

- ☐ Does our data come from a **reliable source**?
- ☐ Does the format of our data display (e.g., table, line graph) help us to **identify similarities, differences, and trends in our data?**
- ☐ Does our data **connect to and support our claim** about how our person/group caused social change?
- ☐ **Explain** why you chose to display your data in this manner and not another.

Toolbox for Change and Tri-fold

Toolbox for Change

Objective: To help show how your issue has evolved and what can be done or has been done to address this need. Your group will create a physical "toolbox for change" that represents what can be used or has been used to create change.

- **Your toolbox must contain at least four items.** For example, if your subject used the legal system to help create change, you might put a gavel in the toolbox, along with three other items. Your items should be symbols of the tools your individual would recommend using.

- **Each item should have a written explanation** that shows how this tool was used and how others could use it, as well.

Get creative! You can use real items or make your own. You can use a shoebox and decorate it, or you can create another vessel that represents your individual.

Tri-fold

Objective: To display your learning in a neat, creative way that will engage visitors. All information should be typed or written neatly.

All three panels should be utilized.

- **Middle Panel:** What we need to do now, how can we do it
- **Side Panel:** Visual presentations of your group's data (charts, graphs, tables, info-graphics) and evidence and analysis of the data for each piece
- **Side Panel:** Pictures, facts about your subject

Along with your **tri-fold**, your **toolbox for change** and a copy of your **essay** will also be displayed.

Exhibition Essay Rubric

	Advanced (4)	Meeting (3)	Approaching (2)	Below (1)	Score
Focus	Introduction has a strong hook and strong essay claim; fits the prompt, task, or topic in an interesting way. Body paragraphs contain accurate, logical paragraph claims and are organized logically. Varied transitions are used to show relationships and enhance the flow of the response. Strong conclusion paragraph fits the topic, introduction, and purpose of the report or essay.	Introduction has a hook and essay claim that clearly fits the prompt, task, or topic. Body paragraphs contain paragraph claims and are organized with reasons and evidence. Transitions fit the report or essay's purpose and help with organization. Solid conclusion paragraph fits the topic, introduction, and purpose of the report or essay.	Introduction shows an attempt at a hook and essay claim. Weak paragraph claims and minimal paragraph organization. Somewhat organized with simple transitions. Weak conclusion paragraph; mostly repeats the introduction.	Introduction missing hook, essay claim unclear. Paragraph claims are unclear or not related; paragraphs seem unorganized. Disorganized; no transitions; transitions not used correctly. No/inappropriate conclusion.	
Use of Evidence	Develops the topic thoroughly by selecting the most significant and relevant facts and data from the text(s). Connection between the evidence and claim is clear and logical. Skillfully integrates data and facts into the text selectively to maintain the flow of ideas and advance the claim. Each body paragraph contains 2 or more pieces of evidence/data from a reliable source.	Develops the topic by selecting relevant facts and data from the text(s). Connection between the evidence and claim is present. Integrates information into the text selectively to maintain the flow of ideas and advance the claim. Each body paragraph contains 2 pieces of evidence/data from a reliable source.	Attempts to develop the topic using facts and data, but it is inaccurate, irrelevant, and/or insufficient. Connection between the evidence and claim is insufficient. Attempts to integrate information into the text selectively to maintain the flow of ideas and advance the claim, but information is insufficient or irrelevant. Each body paragraph contains 1 piece of evidence/data from a reliable source.	Does not develop the topic by selecting information and examples from the text(s). Does not integrate information from the text. Evidence/data is not present or is not evident.	

Exhibition Essay Rubric Continued

	Advanced (4)	Proficient (3)	Basic (2)	Below Basic (1)	Score
Use of Analysis	Skillfully evaluates the prompt and thoughtfully analyzes using original ideas and interpretation of evidence. Skillfully evaluates and interprets data and connects data to overall claim with sophistication. Analysis includes a thoughtful connection to modern-day issue/movement/global problem. Analysis demonstrates a thorough understanding of the complexity of the issue and how it has evolved.	Evaluates the prompt and analyzes using original ideas and interpretation of evidence. Evaluates and interprets data and connects data to overall claim. Analysis includes a connection to modern-day issue/movement/global problem. Analysis demonstrates an understanding of the issue and how it has evolved.	Attempts to evaluate the prompt and analyze how social change was created, but analysis is simple and interpretation of evidence is lacking depth. Analysis includes a superficial attempt to connect to a modern-day movement or issue. Analysis demonstrates a superficial understanding of the issue/global problem.	Does not use evidence from the informational texts to support analysis and/or claim. Does not evaluate the prompt and is missing analysis of the evidence and data provided.	
Style	A variety of simple, compound, and complex sentences. Formal style fits the purpose of the essay; strong voice. Language is skillful, sophisticated, original (doesn't rely on sentence starters).	Different sentence structures; variety in the way sentences begin. Formal style fits the purpose for the essay; voice and tone are evident. Language is clear and appropriate, but may use sentence starters.	Mostly simple sentences or sentences that begin the same way. Formal style needs development; voice and tone not clear. Attempts to use sentence starters, or language may be unclear at times.	Many fragments and/or run-on sentences; several short, choppy sentences. No clear purpose; formal style not present. Language is unclear and sentence starters are not used.	
GMP* *Grammar, Mechanics, Presentation	Minimal, if any, errors in capitalization, usage, punctuation, and spelling; obvious control of the report or essay format. Exceptionally neat; obvious effort to engage the reader. Includes both in-text citations and a works cited page.	Few errors in capitalization, usage, punctuation, and spelling, but they do not interfere with reading or understanding; accurate report or essay format. Correct use of language. Neat, readable. Includes in-text citations for sources and a works cited page.	Some errors in capitalization, usage, punctuation, and spelling that slow down the reader; attempts to create look of a report or an essay. Some problems with language. Not neat; still readable. Missing either in-text citations or a works cited page.	Many errors in capitalization, usage, punctuation, and spelling that interfere with reading; missing look or sense of a report or essay. Shows lack of language skills. Not readable. Missing both in-text citations and a works cited page.	

Toolbox Rubric

	4	3	2	1
Description and Content of Items	4+ items Each item is a thoughtful representation of a tactic used to create change. Each item includes a thoughtful and detailed explanation.	3–4 items Each item is a representation of a tactic used to create change. Each item includes a thoughtful and detailed explanation.	2–3 items Items are a simple representation, literal or very similar in their representation. Simple or missing explanations.	1–2 items Items show minimal thought or detail. Missing explanations.
Creativity	Box itself is creative. Items are creative and show time and effort.	Box itself is simple but effective. Items are simple and effective, showing some thought.	Box itself needed more time and focus. Items are simplistic, needing more time and energy.	Box itself is messy and does not show significant thought. Items are simple, missing thought and detail.

Tri-fold Rubric

	4	3	2	1
Organization, Neatness, & Creativity	The tri-fold is neat and engaging, space is used logically and effectively, *and* it shows creativity.	The tri-fold is neat, engaging, and space is used effectively.	The tri-fold is organized and space is filled, but it could be more engaging, creative, or neat.	The tri-fold appears unorganized or is not engaging to the viewer.
Content	Each section of the tri-fold is present with good detail. There are numerous pictures, facts, and interesting details. There are two pieces of data with thorough explanations. There is a thoughtful connection to and analysis of a modern-day movement.	Each section of the tri-fold is present with sufficient detail. There are pictures, facts, and interesting details. There is at least one piece of data with a thorough explanation. There is a thoughtful connection to a modern-day movement.	Each section of the tri-fold is present but lacks depth or detail . There are a few pictures or facts. There is at least one piece of data, but the explanation may be lacking depth. There is a superficial connection to a modern-day movement.	There is a section missing from the tri-fold, or information is unclear.The board is missing facts or pictures. Data is misleading or missing explanation. The modern-day connection is missing, unconnected, or confusing.

Exhibition Presentation Rubric

	4	3	2	1
Preparedness	Student is completely prepared and has obviously rehearsed.	Student seems pretty prepared but might have needed a couple more rehearsals.	Student is somewhat prepared, but it is clear that rehearsal was lacking.	Student does not seem at all prepared to present.
Comprehension & Content	Student is able to accurately answer almost all questions posed about the topic. Shows a full understanding of the topic.	Student is able to accurately answer most questions posed about the topic. Shows a good understanding of the topic.	Student is able to accurately answer a few questions posed about the topic. Shows a good understanding of parts of the topic.	Student is unable to accurately answer questions posed about the topic. Does not seem to understand the topic very well.
Volume	Volume is loud enough to be heard by all audience members throughout the presentation. Speaks clearly and distinctly all (100%–95%) the time, and mispronounces no words.	Volume is loud enough to be heard by all audience members at least 90% of the time. Speaks clearly and distinctly all (100%–80%) the time, but might mispronounce words.	Volume is loud enough to be heard by all audience members at least 80% of the time. Speaks clearly and distinctly most (80%–60%) of the time. Might mispronounce words.	Volume is often too soft to be heard by all audience members. Often mumbles or cannot be understood.
Collaboration with Peers	Group shares airtime equitably with all presenters.	Group shares airtime most of the time.	Group has a hard time sharing the airtime with all group members.	Group does not share airtime equitably; one member is silent for most of the presentation.
Enthusiasm	Facial expressions and body language generate a strong interest and enthusiasm about the topic in others.	Facial expressions and body language sometimes generate a strong interest and enthusiasm about the topic in others.	Facial expressions and body language are used to try to generate enthusiasm but seem somewhat false.	Very little use of facial expressions or body language. Did not generate much interest in topic being presented.

Independent Social Justice–
Themed Art Project, Senior Year

The Facing History School (FHS) is a small public high school in New York City that was opened in partnership with Facing History and Ourselves in 2005. Students at FHS experience a number of Facing History units and lessons over their four years. All second-semester seniors complete an independent art project that focuses on a social justice topic of personal interest that they have written a paper about during their first semester. The project is self-directed, self-motivated, and explores how to best communicate their message through an interactive art form. Ultimately, the projects are designed to challenge the audience to become upstanders and choose to participate in our changing world.

After completing a brainstorming sheet (included on the following page), with the help of an instructor, students structure their project using a work plan to set up independent deadlines and scaffold the revision process of their art piece. In addition to independent work outside of class, in-class time is spent studying master artwork, peer revising and critiquing proposals and project drafts, working with visiting master artists, and creating their piece. All work is showcased in a Choosing to Participate Final Exhibition at the end of the school year in order to educate staff, students, and community members about the issues they explored during their projects.

Examples of Past FHS Student Art Projects

- Shanequa wanted to eat right but couldn't find places to buy good food in her neighborhood. Out of her observations and frustration, she created a brief film that contrasted the food choices available to people in her neighborhood (KFC, soul food, prepackaged food) to the fresh fruit and vegetables she discovered in mid-town Manhattan. She lamented, "I wanted to understand the reason for so much obesity among African Americans. And now I get it." Her policy recommendation? For every McDonald's, there should be a healthy option. The film featured a tune about obesity and urban living; the singer/songwriter was Shanequa herself.

- Mo, Ashley, Jalil, and Amara chose to focus on police brutality by creating a timeline poster and accompanying painting. "While citizens worry about protecting themselves from criminals, it has now been shown that they must also keep a watchful eye on those who have been given the responsibility to protect and serve them. . . . Police brutality is an important issue to us because people are being treated unfairly and are losing their life due to law enforcement officials taking advantage of their power. . . . We came up with the idea to create a timeline of people who have lost their lives due to police brutality. . . . Our art piece represents how police brutality has always been a problem since slavery days and shows how it is still going on today in our city."

- Ashley used her artistic skills to create a painting that shows how bullying, victim-ization, and discrimination against transgender people is potentially leading to an increase in suicide. "The main message is to advocate for schools to teach gender identity so that students can become accepting of others not like themselves."

This sample project is reproduced with permission from Michael Diaz at the Facing History School, New York, NY.

Choosing to Participate Preparation/ Brainstorming Sheet

What is CTP?

Choosing to Participate is an exhibition of multimedia art projects by The Facing History School's graduating seniors in response to social justice issues. These projects ask you, the audience, to become an upstander and choose to participate in changing our world.

Social issue being addressed:

Will this be a group project? If yes, who is (are) your partner(s)? Are you in the same class?

Description of your social issue:

Why did you choose this topic? Do you have a personal reason for your decision?

Art Project Idea(s):

Group Social Action Project, Senior Year

At Ánimo Jackie Robinson Charter High School in Los Angeles, students also experience Facing History content and themes over four years, developing the vocabulary, skills, and dispositions for effective civic participation and action through many courses. For the culmination of the senior elective Urban Studies/Ethnic Studies, seniors must complete a social action project (SAP) and presentation over the course of two months.

In this case, seniors work in teams of two to four students. The teacher helps students plan and present their projects by structuring the work in phases, starting by identifying and researching issues and then developing an action plan and list of tools, meeting with activists who work on the issue under study, reflecting on the challenges of the project, and finally creating a presentation for classmates, teachers, parents, and community members. During the presentation, seniors share their passion for particular issues, inspirations, challenges and lessons learned, and successes.

The project components include mentor selection, journaling, research, action, presentation, and reflection. After providing an overview of the social action project at the start of the school year, so that students are reflecting on and gathering information about issues—as well as types of and tools for activism—throughout the course, the basic structure of the two-month project is:

- Students self-select groups of 2–4
- Choose a mentor
- Research topics; decide on an area of interest
- Identify a problem
- Come up with a solution
- Identify action tools
- DO SOMETHING
- Reflect on the outcome

Lessons for a Lifetime

"I learned that activism becomes a part of you, a part of your life. That things don't always go the way you plan them, but your job as an activist is to find a way around it and make every effort to make a difference."

—Student, Ánimo Jackie Robinson Charter High School, Los Angeles

Independent Social Action Project, Senior Year

In Connecticut, New Haven Academy students experience Facing History units and content throughout their high school years, including a 9th-grade semester-long course on *Holocaust and Human Behavior*, a 10th-grade semester-long Facing History course, an 11th-grade *Reconstruction Era* unit, and ad hoc advisory lessons. All seniors take a Civics/Choosing to Participate course and complete independent social action projects in their community, culminating in a public presentation at the Senior Exhibition. The goal of these projects is for seniors to learn and practice the skills of active citizenship.

The year-long social action projects (SAP) are facilitated by two teachers and include the student social activists, mentors, partner organizations, and community members. SAP projects can take any form: a rally, a dance, a new website, a public art exhibition, a fundraiser, an after-school program, a party, etc. What is essential is that the students articulate why they believe the format they have chosen is the best way to address their particular issue, meet their goals, and utilize their personal skills.

Project Structure

Although most of the instruction takes place in Civics class, each senior also has a mentor in the fall, school staff member who will keep them on track and meet with them weekly. The mentor coaches, helps, and guides the students, but the students have full ownership of and responsibility for their projects.

A key component of the project is the SAP journal. Each student is required to keep a journal, which is checked regularly by their mentor. The journal is a record of all of the work that they do for their project throughout the year, including reflections, notes, research, interviews, questions, pictures, and an annotated bibliography.

Journal Spotlight

Students are expected to use their journals to document their work and thought process. For example, they are asked to journal on these questions at the start of the project:

Whom do you think you will ask to be your mentor? If this person is unable to be your mentor, whom will you ask? Why, specifically, do you want to ask this person?

Students also reflect as they begin: What are the problems/issues in your community that you might address? Name at least three. What kind of talents or strengths do you think you have? What other questions or concerns do you have?

This sample project is reproduced with permission from Meredith Gavrin and Saul Fussiner at New Haven Academy, New Haven, CT.

Key Elements of the Social Action Projects

- The students choose their issues; the best projects happen when students pursue their passions.
- It is an *action* project, not a research project; they are *doing* something about the issue they choose.
- However, it is *informed* by research; effective social action is guided by a detailed understanding of the problem.
- It gets them out into the community; projects are launched outside the school walls.

Project Portfolio

Every social action project must have the following components in order to be considered complete. Sections must be clearly labeled in students' portfolios (students label with the terms in bold).

1. An approved **SAP Action Plan 1 and 2** (see handouts that follow).
2. **Social action project journal entries** (in *one* "journal doc") that track the progress of the project (journal entries are assigned at specific times, but students are welcome to include additional entries).
3. **Evidence of communication** related to the SAP—emails, notes from phone conversations, notes from meetings.
4. **Research** about the subject, which will be included in the Senior Exhibition (students must include their own annotated texts, notes, and outlines—not unmarked, printed articles).
5. An **annotated bibliography** indicating *all* sources used in the SAP, with commentary about those sources, in proper bibliography format. Students are reminded to add all the sources they have used throughout the year, not just the ones they used for their SAP Action Plan 1.
6. **Visual aids** for the Senior Exhibition (including photographs, sketches, diagrams, graphs, their SAP slide show, and/or other artifacts related to the student's SAP process). It is good to have some images from when the student was participating in the project.

After completing their project, students take part in a Senior Exhibition, where they present their project to the public. Assessment has three parts: Civics class grade, SAP Portfolio (evaluated by the Civics/CTP teacher), and exhibition (evaluated by the audience, including members of the public).

Name: _____   Date _____

SAP Action Plan #1

Your first **Action Plan** for your Social Action Project will be due **November 7**. Presentations to the class will begin that week.

Here is what you need in your Action Plan:

1. **An introduction** that describes the social issue (or problem) you want your SAP to address and explains your interest in the issue; what personal connection, if any, you have to the issue (if one exists and you want to share it); how your interest has developed over time; or any other reasons that have motivated you to commit to this particular issue.

    [Expected length: approximately one page]

2. **Initial research** about your issue: information, ideas, and statistics showing why this problem is important and needs attention. Explain in your own words and quote sources where necessary: How widespread is this problem? Is it growing? How do you know? What are people currently trying to do to address it?

    [Expected length: approximately one page]

3. An **annotated bibliography**. This is a listing of all sources that you used in your research, in MLA or APA format, with a short explanation of what you learned from each one under each entry. *You must have at least three sources.*

    Sample entry and annotation

    Escobedo, T., and Landau, L. "5 Things You Can Do about Climate Change." CNN.com, June 2, 2017, http://www.cnn.com/2017/06/02/us/5-things-you-can-do-about- climate-change/index.html.

    From this web article, I got specific ideas for things people can do in their daily lives for the environment. The article had surprising information about how much of a difference people's actions can make.

4. Your **theory of action**. If I_____ [*the action I plan to take*], then _____ [*the results I hope to see*].

    Example of theory of action: *If I can convince people in my neighborhood to use canvas bags instead of plastic when they shop, then there will be fewer plastic bags killing the marine mammals in Long Island Sound.*

5. Your **project proposal**: Describe your initial plan for your SAP and the form you think your project should take. Based on your research, what do you think is the best way to help address this problem or issue? How can you use your skills, talents, and passions? Who do you want your project to reach or help, and how will you reach them?

[Expected length: 2–3 paragraphs]

Conventions

Typed, 10- or 12-point font
Double-spaced
Proofread; check spelling and grammar
MLA or APA format for annotated bibliography

SAP Action Plan #2

Your second **Action Plan** for your Social Action Project will be due **March 23.**

Section 1: The Details

SAP Action Plan #2 must answer the questions below. You can list the answers (they do not have to be in paragraph form, but please present the information *neatly, clearly, and in detail*).

1. **What is your project?** Explain what you're doing, in 2–3 sentences. Restate your theory of action: "If I _____ [the thing you're doing], then _____ [the results you hope to see, or how that thing will help to address the problem you're trying to help fix].

2. **Where is it taking place?** If it is a physical location, name *the location that has agreed to host you*. If it is online, explain what social media you're using.

3. **When is it taking place?** If it is a one-time event, name *the date you've confirmed*. If it is occurring more than once, list multiple dates. If it's over a period of time, indicate the start and end dates.

4. **Who is the audience?** Who is participating, or who do you hope to reach?

5. **What is the content of the project?** What information, material, or ideas are covered in the project? Be specific and thorough.

6. **What additional tasks do you need to complete in order to be ready to launch the project?**

7. **How did your interview or observation help to inform your work?** If you have not yet connected with anyone in the community for an interview or observation, explain why.

Section 2: The Changes

In full sentences or paragraphs, explain:

- What obstacles have you run into since your first SAP Action Plan?
- What changes have you made to your original plans?
- How do those changes improve your project?

Section 3: The Rubric

Use the SAP rubric to assess your own work on your SAP thus far; grade yourself **and write comments** to explain the grading.

Final Section: Appendices

Attach *at least two* items you've created for your project so far. Everyone will have something different, but some examples might include:

- A design for the homepage of the website you're creating (or the actual link if it's live)
- A one-page proposal you created to convince someone to host your project
- Lesson plans for classes you're teaching, or an agenda for a workshop or panel discussion
- Flyers/posters advertising your project
- Drafts of scripts, lyrics, dialogue, film storyboard (for creative projects)
- Other items or documents you've created for your project

Conventions

Typed, 10- or 12-point font
Double spaced
Proofread; check spelling and grammar
NOTE: In order to meet the deadline, *all* of the pieces have to be submitted on time.

Additional Resources

The following educational resources—in addition to a wide range of lessons, units, study guides, primary source documents, streaming videos, and more materials designed to support social studies, history, humanities, civics, and English language arts educators—can be found at **facinghistory.org**.

Back-to-School Toolkit

This one-week unit is designed to develop students' social–emotional skills during the first days of the semester, in order to engage in an open and supportive classroom community. Lessons help teachers establish classroom norms and an inclusive environment where students honor and value differing perspectives, question assumptions, and actively listen to others.

Fostering Civil Discourse: A Guide for Classroom Conversation

Provides strategies to support your students as they develop effective skills for civic participation. Also check out the two-part webinar series in our On-Demand Learning Center (facinghistory.org/ondemand).

My Part of the Story: Exploring Identity in the United States

Designed to launch a course about US history, literature, or civic life through an examination of students' individual identities. When students explore and define their identities and their relationship to society, they are empowered to develop their voice and their ability to participate in respectful dialogue, deliberation, and reflection.

Teaching Current Events

Exploring current events is fundamental to civics because current events introduce the issues, dilemmas, and controversies that shape civic life today, empower students to make informed choices and take meaningful action, and foster key civic skills. Check out Facing History's teaching ideas and explainers for addressing breaking news and ongoing issues, checklists of things to consider before you start teaching current events, and strategies for navigating partisan politics in diverse classrooms (facinghistory.org/current-events).

Community Matters

Built on a foundation of social and emotional learning, this advisory curriculum for grades 8–10 provides a year's worth of activities and materials designed to help educators build student-centered spaces where honest questioning, discussion, and social and academic growth can occur. The curriculum also aims to build civic agency and includes guidelines for a community-building CTP project designed to benefit the school community.

Core Case Studies

These units are designed using the Facing History and Ourselves scope and sequence; most include a Choosing to Participate chapter, readings, or lessons. Some of them also include a supplement with specific writing prompts that require students to gather evidence from that unit's rich collection of primary source documents, use that evidence to make claims about the past, and craft a formal argumentative essay.

- Choices in Little Rock
- Civil Rights Historical Investigations
- Crimes against Humanity and Civilization: The Genocide of the Armenians
- The Nanjing Atrocities: Crimes of War
- Race and Membership in American History: The Eugenics Movement
- The Reconstruction Era and the Fragility of Democracy
- Standing Up for Democracy
- Stolen Lives: The Indigenous Peoples of Canada and the Indian Residential Schools
- Teaching *Holocaust and Human Behavior*
- Teaching *Mockingbird*

CPSIA information can be obtained
at www.ICGtesting.com
Printed in the USA
JSHW030812150520
5699JS00007B/34